A Son of Taiwan

A Son of Taiwan

Stories of Government Atrocity

EDITED BY

Howard Goldblatt and Sylvia Li-chun Lin

Literature from Taiwan Series
in collaboration with
the National Museum of Taiwan Literature,
National Taiwan Normal University, and
the National Human Rights Museum
General Editor: Nikky Lin

Amherst, New York

Copyright 2021 Cambria Press,
the National Museum of Taiwan Literature,
and the National Human Rights Museum.

All rights reserved.
No part of this publication may be reproduced, stored in or introduced into a retrieval system, or transmitted, in any form, or by any means (electronic, mechanical, photocopying, recording, or otherwise), without the prior permission of the publisher.

Requests for permission should be directed to
permissions@cambriapress.com, or mailed to:
Cambria Press
100 Corporate Parkway, Suite 128
Amherst, New York 14226, USA

Front cover image is *The House of Yang Kui* by Huang Jung-tsan.

Library of Congress Cataloging-in-Publication Data

Names: Goldblatt, Howard, 1939- editor. | Lin, Sylvia Li-chun, editor.

Title: A son of Taiwan : stories of government atrocity / edited by Howard Goldblatt and Sylvia Li-chun Lin.

Description: Amherst, New York : Cambria Press, [2021] | Series: Literature from Taiwan |
Summary: "On February 28, 1947, a widow selling cigarettes on the street in Taipei was brutally beaten by government agents searching for contraband cigarettes. When a crowd gathered, shots were fired and a bystander was killed. Island-wide demonstrations prompted the Chiang Kai-shek government to send reinforcements from China. Upon arrival, the troops opened fire, killing thousands. The massacre was followed by large-scale arrests of anyone suspected of sedition or Communist associations, all in the name of national security. Martial law was declared and not lifted until 1987. What happened in 1947 is known as the 2/28 Incident, which led to a four-decade-long suppression of dissent, encroachments upon civil liberties, and the wholesale violation of human rights, all subsumed under an era referred to as White Terror. Its pernicious effects went beyond actual acts of atrocity, as the citizens practiced self-censorship and passed their fears on to the next generation. For many years, this part of Taiwan's past was talked about, if at all, with circumspection. As evidenced in this collection, literary representations often employed obscure references, which themselves could place the writers in serious jeopardy. Despite, or because of, differences in approach, these writers keep memories alive to ensure that the past is neither forgotten nor repeated. This book is part of the Literature from Taiwan Series, in collaboration with the National Museum of Taiwan Literature and National Taiwan Normal University"-- Provided by publisher.

Identifiers: LCCN 2021002334 (print) | LCCN 2021002335 (ebook) | ISBN 9781621966937 (paperback) | ISBN 9781621965947 (pdf) | ISBN 9781621965954 (epub)

Subjects: LCSH: Short stories, Chinese--Taiwan.

Classification: LCC PL3031.T32 S68 2021 (print) | LCC PL3031.T32 (ebook) | DDC 895.13/01080951249--dc23

LC record available at https://lccn.loc.gov/2021002334

LC ebook record available at https://lccn.loc.gov/2021002335

Table of Contents

Foreword vii

Note from Series Editor ix

Introduction: Stories of Taiwan
    Sylvia Li-chun Lin 1

1: Potsdam Section Chief
    Wu Zhuoliu (translated by Sylvia Li-chun Lin and Howard Goldblatt) 9

2: Jian A-tao
    Ye Shitao (translated by Craig A. Smith) 69

3: Red Dragonfly
    Lay Chih-ying (translated by Darryl Sterk) 103

4: Auntie Tiger
    Li Ang (translated by Jewel Lo and Dafydd Fell) 113

5: Nocturnal Strings
    Lee Yu (translated by Chris Wen-chao Li) 143

6: Cruelty of the City
    Walis Nokan (translated by Edward Vickers) 177

About the Authors 197

About the Editors and Translators 199

Cambria Literature in Taiwan Series 203

Foreword

Taiwanese literature, like its history, reflects the island's hybrid ethnic diversity and unique culture. Due to its geographical proximity to the Chinese Empire, Taiwanese literature has been greatly influenced by the ancient tradition of classical Chinese literature.

In 1895, Taiwan's fifty-one years of Japanese colonial rule began. During this period, the groundwork for the development of modern Taiwanese literature was laid. The end of World War II also meant the end of Japanese rule, but it was not a time of peace for Taiwan, which found itself caught in the escalation of the Cold War. The result of this was thirty-eight years of martial law. However, through political activism and the persistent efforts of the Taiwanese people who sought to revolutionize and refine the island's political system, martial law ended in 1987 and the island was transformed into Asia's most liberal country, and one with a strong, democratic political system. The struggle for democracy also set the tone for increased responsiveness and acceptance in the literary sphere.

As such, it is important that the world learns about the distinctive brand into which Taiwan literature has evolved. This book is part of the Literature from Taiwan Series, which comprises a varied selection of literary works showcasing exemplary Taiwan literature. It is part of a systematic and measured attempt to introduce Taiwan's distinctiveness to the rest of the world.

All the literary creations featured in the series have been composed by writers who were afflicted or confined by the societal pressures of their time. If one reads a single work of Taiwanese literature, one can easily sense the exuberance of Taiwan's literary masters. However, when one reads a collection, one can experience the force that is driving Taiwan forward.

Since the Taiwan Ministry of Culture's launch of its promotional project, "Books From Taiwan (BFT)" in 2016, the Taiwanese Ministry of Culture has taken on a proactive role in establishing an international copyright information platform and has been an active presence at international book fairs. The Ministry of Culture, furthermore, has been inviting international translators to Taiwan and assisting in the facilitation of translations of Taiwanese books into various languages, measures which have proven fruitful thus far. The National Museum of Taiwan Literature (NMTL) is affiliated with the Ministry of Culture and its structural organization/structural mechanism aligns with that of the BFT, with both parties focusing on the promotion of important Taiwan literary creations.

In addition to this book series, the NMTL has been working on creating a long-term database of translators of Taiwanese literature. It has also conducted a Taiwanese literary survey in various countries with the aim of promoting Taiwanese literature internationally as well as raising awareness for Taiwan's literary excellence, thus giving it a well-deserved voice on the international stage of world literature.

—Su Shuo-Bin,
Director,
National Museum of Taiwan Literature

Note from Series Editor

The image on this book's front cover is The House of Yang Kui (1947) by Huang Jung-tsan. Born in Chongqing in 1916, Huang Jung-tsan settled in Taiwan in 1945. His works are renowned for their skillful documentation of the lives of the working class. The artist himself became embroiled in Taiwan's White Terror and was shot in 1952. The painting is a visual depiction of the social activist and liberal writer Yang Kui, highlighting his perseverance and the hardships suffered during Taiwan's authoritarian era.

I would like to thank Yi-Chia Lee, Kirsten Klitsch, and Chein-Sen Peng for their assistance on this project.

—Nikky Lin,
General Editor,
Literature from Taiwan Series

A Son of Taiwan

Introduction

Stories of Taiwan

Sylvia Li-chun Lin

The stories in this collection are set in the 1940s and 1950s, but to understand and appreciate their significance, we must travel back to 1895, when Taiwan was ceded to Japan by the Qing court in the wake of a resounding defeat in the Sino-Japanese War. The colonial takeover ignited fierce fighting by the Taiwanese, including members of the intelligentsia, who would continue their resistance throughout the colonial period, but to no avail. Taiwan initially did not suffer to the same degree as Korea, which Japan ruled ruthlessly. Nevertheless, the Taiwanese were regarded as second-class citizens, discriminated against, and denigrated by the Japanese colonials. When the Pacific War broke out, Taiwanese were forced to adopt Japanese names and lifestyles, and Japanese was formalized as the island's official language. Predictably, Taiwanese eagerly awaited the arrival of those from the Motherland at the end of World War II.

Their joy was short-lived and anticipation dashed when the islanders began to feel the effects of economic disruption and social unrest, some of which was the inevitable aftermath of war, while much of it was precipitated by the new arrivals. Taiwan was, in a word, a powder keg. On February 28, 1947, a widow selling cigarettes on the street in Taipei was brutally beaten up by government agents searching for contraband goods. When a crowd gathered, shots were fired and a bystander was killed. The percolating discontent finally boiled over, leading to massive island-wide demonstrations, which then prompted the Chiang Kai-shek government to send reinforcements from China. Upon arrival, the troops opened fire, killing thousands of residents. The massacre was followed by large-scale arrests of anyone suspected of sedition or Communist associations. Martial law was declared, not to be lifted until July 15, 1987.

What happened in 1947 has come to be known as the 2/28 or February 28 Incident, which led to a four-decade-long suppression of dissent, encroachments upon civil liberties, and the wholesale violation of human rights, all subsumed under an era referred to as White Terror. In the name of national security, thousands were arrested, their innocence notwithstanding, and many were "disappeared" by agents of the notorious Garrison Command. The pernicious effects of White Terror went beyond actual acts of atrocity, as the citizens practiced self-censorship and passed their fears on to the next generation. For many years, this part of Taiwan's past was talked about, if at all, with circumspection as the overriding principle. Literary representations often employed obscure references, which themselves could get the writers into serious trouble, or worse.

After the lifting of martial law, despite internal and external obstacles, Taiwan gradually evolved into the first true Asian democracy, a political and cultural milieu in which Taiwanese no longer had to tiptoe around sensitive topics. A great deal of historical research has been undertaken on this turbulent period, the results published and widely read. The stories in this collection, though fictional in nature, expand our understanding of Taiwan's postcolonial history and extend our memory of the past, in Taiwan's pursuit of transitional justice.

In order to present a linear macro-story of this period, we have opted for chronological order of the historical background against which the stories are set. The writers included vary greatly in age difference—from the oldest, Wu Zhuoliu (b. 1900) to the youngest, Lay Chih-ying (b. 1981). Some lived through the colonial period and a greater part of the martial-law era, which enabled them to write from personal experience, while younger writers like Lai came of age after the lifting of martial law and have had to rely on historical documents and the recorded experiences of earlier generations. Despite their age differences, these writers keep memories alive through their works to ensure that the past is neither forgotten nor repeated.

The first selection, "Potsdam Section Chief" by Wu Zhuoliu, is set in the period immediately after the war ended, when official personnel from China came to take over properties left behind by the Japanese. It features a well-educated Taiwanese woman, Yulan, whose longing for the motherland is projected onto Fan Hanzhi. She discovers, however, soon after their wedding, that he is a vulgar, shallow man who is interested only in fattening his wallet. In the end she is disillusioned, as were the Taiwanese. The author clearly intended for their marriage to symbolize the relationship between Taiwan and China, which makes the ending of the story both intriguing and significant.

The second piece includes four excerpts from Ye Shitao's *Jian A-tao, A Son of Taiwan*. "The Sad Story of Luku" is a semi-autobiographical story based on the five years Ye spent in prison for not reporting on suspected communists. In addition to a vivid description of the life of political prisoners, the story obliquely refers to a real-life incident that took place in Luku, when in 1952 an entire village was arrested on trumped-up charges. "My Days of Eating Pork Skin" and "Encounter" focus on the protagonist's life after his release; shunned by friends and unable to find a job, he is reduced to menial labor and lives in perpetual dejection. "The

Interrogation" puts Jian A-tao back into the clutches of the secret police, which views a former political prisoner as forever suspicious.

"Red Dragonfly," by the youngest writer in this collection, is set in the immediate aftermath of the 2/28 Incident, during which the narrator's cousin, also his best friend, was "disappeared." Later, the narrator, now a medical school student, sees his cousin on a dissecting table as a cadaver. As we follow the progression of the dissection, we learn about the left-leaning cousin and his friendship with Lü Heruo, a real-life character who perished during the early years of the White Terror era. We do not learn what the cousin did to deserve his fate, but guilt by association was a singular trait of the era; one need not have committed an act of sedition to be charged, even executed.

It is not an overstatement to say that ambiguity was a necessary narrative technique in literary works when representing atrocities in Taiwan. For one thing, this part of Taiwan's past came to light only after the lifting of martial law, and even then a great deal of research was required to unearth the past, however fragmented the results might have been. Those who were in the midst of unfolding events were often oblivious to just what was happening, like the narrator in "Red Dragonfly." For another, during the martial-law period, writers needed to be discreet in their portrayals of these taboos. Lee Yu's "Nocturnal Strings" is an apt example. Employing an elliptical narrative style, Lee presents a woman whose husband was "disappeared" by the government. Readers must piece together the hints inserted here and there to understand the protagonist's life, very much in the same way later generations have learned about Taiwan's past. The husband's eventual execution for being a suspected Communist is suggested only through a reference to the execution site at the end of the story. Significantly, the characters are not native Taiwanese, thus giving the concept of "victimization" greater breadth. Published in 1986 by an author who was placed on the KMT's blacklist, the story exemplifies the utilization of textual and extra-textual secrecy.

That the 2/28 Incident led to the oppressive era of White Terror has been generally acknowledged, though the latter was mainly manifested in the arrest of suspected communists. Viewed thus, Li Ang's "Auntie Tiger" is a connecting story in the larger narrative of the period. Xie Xuehong, the protagonist and a real-life character, was a card-carrying member of the Taiwanese Communist party. Her activities during and after the 2/28 Incident originated from her belief in the promise of communism, which eventually led to her exile to China. True to Li Ang's multifaceted talent, "Auntie Tiger" is not merely the re-creation of a Taiwanese woman's life against the historical backdrop; rather, it also incorporates gossip and the well-known Taiwanese folktale, Auntie Tiger, to destabilize historical records and expose gender bias against women in politics.

The three short stories from *Cruelty of the City* by Walis Nokan center on the life of the Yuanzhumin under the authoritarian regime. Ranging from the persecution of a tribal elder by the Garrison Command to the satirical treatment of an absurd ritual of saluting Chiang Kai-shek's statue to the thorny of issue of betrayal under duress, these stories not only confirm that the net of terror was indeed cast far and wide, but also showcase the author's unique narrative voice and styles. As a tiny minority, the Austronesian native segment of Taiwan's population (less than three percent), the Yuanzhumin and their experience are seldom mentioned. These excerpts of a work by Walis Nokan help to rectify a slight that is all too common in societies where the majority speaks the loudest.

A few words on the cover: *Yang Kuei's Room*, a woodblock print by Huang Rongcan. Both the artist and his subject exemplify the topics covered in this collection. Huang Rongcan (1916–1952) was born in Chongqing, Sichuan. An accomplished woodblock print artist, he was active in the art world in China and participated in the war against Japan through his creative activities. A considerable number of his works were included in Pearl Buck's *China In Black & White* and have become part of the permanent collections at the British Museum and the National

Gallery of Australia, among others. He arrived in Taiwan in the winter of 1945. After personally experiencing the 1947 massacre, he created vivid portrayals that bear witness to the atrocity. He was arrested in 1952 on a groundless charge of sedition and executed on November 19 at the spot mentioned in Lee Yu's story. During his brief sojourn in Taiwan, he mentored and nurtured a new generation of Taiwanese artists, including Yang Ying-feng.

Yang Kuei (1906–1985) was a Taiwanese intellectual and writer whose life-long fight against authoritarian state apparatuses led to ten arrests by the Japanese colonial government and imprisonment totaling forty-five days. He and his wife, Yeh Tao, were arrested by the Chiang Kai-shek regime in 1947 and barely escaped execution. A year later he was arrested for drafting a peace declaration, for which he took full responsibility and was given a twelve-year sentence. In 1951 he was sent to Green Island to serve out his incarceration and was not released until 1961. He never ceased writing or fighting.

During the editing process, we encountered terms that deserve additional treatment. First and foremost is "retrocession," which refers to the ceding of Taiwan by Japan to Chiang Kai-shek's government, formalized in the 1943 Cairo Conference. It is not an ideal term, for it runs up against a different interpretation of Taiwanese history. For some, Taiwan was a Japanese colony that was later ceded to the Nationalist government. Therefore, instead of referring to the political change of 1945 as Taiwan being retroceded to the Nationalist government, they advocate designating the event as "the end of World War II." Taiwan's status vis-à-vis Japan has also created disparate terminology, some preferring to call Taiwan "Japan's colony," while others insist on the "Japanese occupation" of Taiwan. These are volatile political issues. As editors, we prefer to remain neutral and instead focus on the merits of the collection. But choose we must, so retrocession has to do, and we have opted for "colonial period," rather than "occupation." It is impossible to to please all, but we believe it is a good compromise. The pinyin spelling system, now common in Taiwan, has been used throughout, except for established spellings of some personal names and major cities.

We thank the translators, most of whom sent their work and responded to queries in a timely fashion. The schedule was tight, but together we got it done. Discussing terms, word usage, meaning, and style with the translators was enjoyable and fruitful, further affirming why we do what we do. Our thanks to Professor Nikky Lin of Taiwan Normal University for giving us this opportunity and for choosing the stories and translators on which we worked. Thanks also to Cambria Press, whose editors worked hard to present the stories in the best shape possible.

1

POTSDAM SECTION CHIEF

Wu Zhuoliu
(translated by Sylvia Li-chun Lin and Howard Goldblatt)

Preface

The Potsdam Declaration can be considered the greatest event of the twentieth century, for it was made at a time when billions of people around the world were shedding blood and tears in a frenzied fight for survival.

Some good did indeed come of it, such as the Potsdam General, the Potsdam Statesman, plus Dr. Potsdam, Professor Potsdam, Potsdam Parvenu, Chairman Potsdam, and so on. Our Potsdam Section Chief was one of them. He might have looked and sounded like everyone else, but there was no doubt about his status as an historical product worthy of celebration.

Author's note, Oct. 8, 1947

1

"Have you heard, Director?" Fan Hanzhi hollered as he stormed through the door from the sweltering oven outside.

"Heard what?" Department Director Peng replied with a visible lack of interest. He looked up while putting the cigarette he'd just removed back between his lips.

"The Japanese have surrendered."

"What? The Japanese surrendered?"

"Yes. It was just announced."

"Oh." Peng sighed heavily and continued, his lips quivering, "I never expected the Japanese to be so worthless, totally unreliable."

His face turned ashen, betraying his mental state.

He'd known this day would come, just not so soon. When anticipation turned into reality, what he'd waited for lost its meaning. Now he was at a loss, apprehensive and rattled, unsure what to do next. Peng was not the only person in the office who felt that way. His weak-willed colleagues blanched, their faces shrouded in a ghastly gray pall. Fan Hanzhi was the only one who kept his composure, true to his position as chief of the secret service section. The panicky look on Peng's face reminded Fan of something. Imagining himself sticking out his tongue, he said,

"What's the point of sighing now, Director? No need to worry about anything but the money. Let's divide up the public funds and earnings, and clear out of here."

"Ah, you're right, of course, but isn't it a bit too soon? We haven't heard anything from the Central Government."

"The Central Government? Waiting for those pains in the neck will make us all sitting ducks. Chongqing has sent over plenty of its undercover agents. If we're not careful and we get caught, we'll be labeled traitors for sure."

A glance at the Department Director's face told Fan his boss had lost the ability to decide on a proper course of action, like a rudderless boat. Fan was secretly pleased that his plan was working out well; he didn't care about anything but getting his hands on the money. He knew he must convince Peng, so he said more forcefully,

"You're too soft, Director. You'll have no way out if you don't make up your mind, and do it fast. The Central Government is coming, and once lost, this opportunity . . ."

After another look at Peng, Fan changed his tone and issued an order,

"Give me the key, Director."

A different man now, Peng handed over the critical item. Fan opened the safe and pulled out the gold bars and cash, laying them out on the desk.

"This portion goes to Director Peng, this to the Chief of First Section, then Chief of Second Section, and this is my share. Come and get it." Fan pointed at the piles as he stuffed his share into two large leather cases. Then he said to the wavering director and section chiefs,

"So long."

He got into his car and drove off.

"Bloody fools. They're in for it now, the idiots."

He said this to himself as a sly smile bloomed on his face. He'd settled his family and valuables in Shanghai in preparation for his flight for just such a critical moment.

Fan worked in the secret service section of the Inspector General's office. A clever and ruthless man, he was nevertheless little known to society, for he worked behind the scenes. He knew he would be safe once he was out of Nanjing. No one would accuse him of being a traitor, a concern he put out of his mind once he'd driven through Zhonghua Gate. Instead, he glanced at the two cases and said to himself,

"This will be enough for me to live on for the next ten, maybe twenty, years. I'd be a fool to get caught as a traitor."

The car continued tearing down the street under a mid-summer sun whose bright light glinted off pebbles. As a wind blew in through the window, he soothed his conscience with the common expression that victors become leaders while losers are considered outlaws. And yet something still didn't feel right to him, a thought that festered for a while until he forced himself to think about his future in Shanghai.

"Nothing to worry about," he said to himself. "With all this I'll be ..."

One day, a couple of months later, he happened upon a newspaper story about traitors, one that included Director Peng and his colleagues. A quick count told him they'd all been arrested. "Pity those who aren't smart enough." He couldn't help feeling sorry for them. After reading it a few more times, he turned to the news item beneath it, where the words "taking over Taiwan" caught his eye.

"Of course. I completely forgot about that treasure island. How careless of me. Taiwan, a bountiful island, with two rice harvests a year. Everything grows there, and they have salt, camphor, tea, bananas, oranges, sugar. Ah, sugar. Bringing the sugar back here would mean ..."

His eyes were fixed on the report while the wheels in his head continued to turn.

2

Baking in the autumn heat, Yulan looked at the long line snaking outside the Governor General's Office. Gongs and drums raised a din that added to the noise of the crowd. Student organizations, the Three People's Principle Youth Corps, and a lion-dance troupe marched behind banners celebrating the Retrocession of Taiwan. It was truly festive. The long procession of celebrants included Taoist guards Generals Fan and Xie, as well as musical instruments with a strong Chinese flavor that had virtually disappeared over the past decade or so. The effects of fifty years of the Japanese Kominka Movement seemed to have vanished overnight.

The streets were thronged with people, young and old, men and women, and abuzz with everyone in an elated, celebratory mood. On both sides of the street by the Governor General's Office stood silent rows of Japanese middle-school, girls-school, and high-school students. The sight shook Yulan. These were the same people who had disdainfully and smugly called the Taiwanese "Chinamen." Seeing how they were now, she felt sorry for them, especially because of their sad expressions. "I wonder how the Japanese feel now." But it was too noisy for her to continue her thoughts, and she felt like a child who missed her mother. She couldn't wait to see soldiers from the Motherland, but she'd been waiting such a long time and still no sign of them. All she saw was the welcoming procession snaking past in front of her. Her feet were growing numb.

Losing patience, she kept walking out into the street to get a better look, but there were no soldiers in sight. Waiting, she realized, was excruciating.

The scorching autumn sun was so harsh it stung her skin. But then, after three or four hours, the army from the Motherland finally arrived. A deafening roar erupted, and waves of cheers seemed never-ending. Everyone was waving flags, so many their undulating waves blocked her view, forcing her to stand on tiptoe to see.

The line of soldiers seemed interminable, each soldier carrying an umbrella over his back, a sight that puzzled Yulan. But she blotted out her bewilderment and told herself it was just something she hadn't seen before. Some were also carrying iron woks, utensils, and bedrolls, which reminded her of what she'd seen as a child, when Taiwanese theater troupes moved on to new performing sites. She was disappointed, but, with the Japanese nearby, she refused to let her emotions show. She wasn't being biased; it was just a matter of self-esteem, something coursing through her veins that even she could not explain. It was like having a wish suddenly granted, and though what she got was flawed, she still could not suppress a sense of satisfaction. Without knowing it, tears welled in her eyes, as she felt like an adopted child finally meeting birth parents, even if they were beggars.

"Hey! They're here. The soldiers from the Motherland are here."

She was filled with indescribable joy, her greedy eyes fixed on the marchers' receding backs. When she turned to look behind her, she saw that the crowds, all wearing happy smiles, were slowly dispersing.

They carried her along. Still at the height of their excitement, everyone was talking and gesturing as they walked off. Naturally, she heard everything they said.

"Carrying an umbrella like that, it's a bit, well, you know."

"But it isn't just an umbrella. It's a weapon that also comes in handy when it rains. And they can use it on the battlefield when they jump down from higher ground," someone confidently explained.

"Are you saying our soldiers can fly?"

"Of course, they can. Can't you see the iron rings around their ankles? Don't they look bigger than the Japanese soldiers' leggings?"

"Ah, I see."

"They walk with heavy rings around the ankles, so when they're removed, they can leap across wide gulches. They can even jump over city walls, easy."

The know-it-all went on and on, impressing everyone around him. Yulan was dubious, but she had to wonder if victory would have been possible if the soldiers hadn't had rigorous training.

At school, she'd been taught to be a good Japanese, but she never could, no matter how hard she tried. She'd learned how to wash her face and dress herself, but the kimono always felt unnatural. Besides, she'd often heard her classmates talk about her:

"Look at her. She may have adopted a Japanese name, but see how ridiculous she looks in her kimono?"

She had endured such emotional corrosion for a long time, but now she could rid herself of it all. The realization buoyed her mood.

Taiwan had been under Japanese rule for fifty years, and every Taiwanese had grown up as a child without a Motherland. On countless occasions, she'd had to lower her head in debased self-esteem before the Japanese, who had a Motherland to pride themselves in. And now, she didn't ever have to do that again.

"Ah, I'm so lucky. I should be enormously grateful. I'd join the army to protect our country if I were a man."

Being born female felt like a huge privation. But on second thought, women could do something for the country, too. In any case, knowing Mandarin was the key, and she made up her mind, "I'll do my best, I'll learn Mandarin. That's what I'll do."

She had nothing to do at home, and being idle was no fun.

Everyone else was still reveling in the postwar jubilation as she made up her mind to study Mandarin on her own.

The phonetic symbols were easy enough to learn, but the sounds that required curling her tongue, which were not present in Taiwanese and Japanese, were a challenge. Even so, she could greet and carry on simple conversations after a couple of months' effort. Now she tried her Mandarin on everyone she met.

3

Once spring arrived, with its balmy weather, Yulan could not just sit around the house, so she decided to take a break and go into town. On Wenwu Street, she noticed a great many women in qipaos, which, with their soft curves, symbolized a new sensation, and were especially eye-catching. Her attention was also drawn to young couples holding hands. Everything and everywhere she looked was filled with peace and beauty. She had to admire the swift changes in society and felt she might fall behind if she didn't pay attention.

She crossed over to another street. Under the overhang and on every empty spot Japanese were selling their furniture at makeshift stalls. All used items, nothing new in sight. There were beautiful kimonos too, but she was in no mood to look at them now. People who'd come in from the countryside, however, were gushing over the low prices and buying up even tattered clothes, as the long war had created a severe shortage of material items.

Eventually tiring from the walk, she entered a café and ordered a coffee. The gramophone was still playing coquettish Japanese music.

Before long, a young man floated in. In his early thirties, he was dressed in a neatly pressed Shanghai-style suit and a bright red tie. He stood in the doorway and surveyed the café before taking an empty seat by Yulan with a ceremonious air. As if feeling pressured, she lowered her head and took a sip of coffee when she heard the young man order black tea in fluent Mandarin. The waitress could not understand him, so he wrote it out for her.

Then he looked at Yulan flirtatiously, making her so uncomfortable she wanted to finish as quickly as possible and leave. But he spoke to her in a somewhat formal manner:

"May I know your name, Miss?" he asked.

"My family name is Zhang." she said, tilting her head.

She'd stammered her reply, this being the first time she'd actually used Mandarin in a conversation. Something felt lodged in her throat. With that exchange breaking the ice, he continued with his questions. Yulan was shy at first and tongue-tied, but it got better, and she was pleased by the ability to share her views with him.

He was cordial, without the gruffness common among Taiwanese young men. She was impressed by his fluent, easily understandable Mandarin as well as his refined, polite manner. Half an hour quickly passed as they talked. Yulan came under the spell of the Mainland man.

4

Yulan was ill at ease when another Sunday rolled around. She opened her book to study Mandarin, but her thoughts ran away to the tea shop. The image of the Shanghai-style young man flashed past her mind's eye, and she could almost hear him whispering to her in Mandarin. She'd like to talk to him again, a thought that made her blush; there was no one around, but she felt bashful and somewhat frightened.

Calming her agitated mind, she tried to read, but the words in the book seemed to have grown thorns to prevent her understanding. She closed the book, rested her chin on her hand, and let her thoughts wander. Her gaze fell on the profuse peach and plum blooms in the yard, where butterflies flitted in pairs among the flowers. The soft rays of the sun shone on them gently, reminding her of Beitou and Grass Mountain, where the scenery at this moment must be enchanting. She recalled what she'd missed most about her school days, when she'd drive out there with her best friends during the peach blossom season. Scenes from the past replayed before her like images on a carousel lantern.

But friends from those days were all housewives now. Her thoughts turned to Xiuzi, whom she'd run into a few days earlier. Her friend was holding a baby and strutting down the street arm in arm with her husband. Yulan was besieged by loneliness stemming from her unsettled life, as an emotional sigh burst out of her mature body.

"Ah, Spring is almost over, and I haven't yet gone to take a look at all the flowers."

She felt her blood surge, something she'd never dreamed could happen, and lamented how the flowers seemed to have bloomed for nothing during such splendid times. She sang silently,

"Everything is so lovely, so charming, and yet I am all alone. Ai . . ."

Her spacious bedroom felt empty, no place for her to either sit still or move about in. If only she could have kept reading, but the book had lost its appeal. Her head felt stuffy, and her young heart had plunged into a deep chasm, where it bobbed in violent, emotional turbulence. She did her best to suppress feelings that refused to be quelled. It was noon before she knew it, and she sank more deeply into troubled thoughts.

Out of the blue, the man she'd met at the café appeared. Naturally, she did not know that he was Fan Hanzhi, who had fled the Mainland, for he had changed his name and buried his past. As Fan Xinsheng now, he had managed to obtain a position as an accounting section chief at some bureau, a feat no one could have imagined possible.

Yulan was happy to see him. Under the spell of her longing for the Motherland, she was predisposed to like him, the end result of her latent yearning, an emotion she could not understand, one she was not even aware of.

"I apologize for my behavior the other day. I'm new here and don't know anyone. I have no place to go on Sundays, so I took the liberty of coming to visit you."

He explained his sudden appearance in fluent Mandarin. His manner showed his social skills, and his hair was combed neatly, his suit was crease-free, all of which made him appear even more urbane and striking. Gruff Taiwanese young men could not hope to be his equal in the prudent, modest way he talked, and, in particular, his genial tone when speaking to a woman. That alone made her feel that he was both approachable and reliable. She was impressed by his abundant conversational topics, especially about the new Shanghai women, how dynamic they were. She envied them.

"My English is terrible. I studied it in school, but I only know 'yes' and 'no.' I could never go to Shanghai."

"Of course, you can. With a good foundation, you'll learn quickly once you're there. But let's not talk about that now. There are three things people rave about: Chinese food, Western buildings, and Japanese wives. Back in the Motherland, everyone says Japanese women make the best wives. But now that I'm here, I can see what the students returning from Japan have said was true. Taiwanese women, in particular, are more talented and graceful, since they retain the culture of the Motherland with the additional influence of a Japanese education."

She was enormously pleased by his praise. Fan smiled cunningly when he saw the expected result of what he'd said. But he did not forget to hide his true feelings, so as not to leave a negative impression. Knowing not to overstay his welcome, he took his leave.

After he walked out, Fan said to himself: "Taiwanese women lack sophistication and are pleasingly straightforward; they might be fragile emotionally, but they're innocent to the point of being naïve, which means I can do what I want with them."

His mood brightened dramatically by the analysis. When he looked up and saw the colorful sunset above Datun shan, his heart stirred with fanciful thoughts.

The following Sunday was the day he'd waited for all week. He dashed off to call on Yulan with a gift. She had recently been liberated from the terrifying life of leaving everything behind to hide daily in a shelter under the threat of an air strike. After the retrocession, she was like a lamb that had escaped the abattoir to graze freely on grassland under a clear blue sky. And yet, once the calm life went on a bit longer, dissatisfaction set in and she needed some excitement in her life. Her emotions were at a fever pitch. Spring was here, but she could not feel the repose of the season and instead was plagued by an unshakable vexation. Without intending to, she thought about the meaning of "life."

Time had passed quickly, and she was already twenty-six, nearly time for a flower to wilt. She felt like a pot of flowers, withering before drawing dancing butterflies or singing birds. Ah. Life really was like a dream. But what was its purpose?

She spotted a pair of doves pecking outside. They hopped all around close together, their feathers reflecting the soft sunlight of springtime and giving off a pleasant sheen. They then flew off into the azure sky. Humans aren't as free as birds, are they?

She'd once gone to the hot springs on Grass Mountain with some school friends. It had been a day just like this, with flowers blooming in a gentle breeze under a bright sun. They'd shared a picnic near the flowers at noon, close to a group of young men under a tree. One of them had come over and asked for a cup of tea. He'd pushed his military cap up, almost flirtatiously. The tea thermos shook as she poured, and she felt herself burning up. But she didn't see him again until one day after graduation. She was shopping at Rongding, when she spotted him, wearing a red sash over his neatly pressed army uniform. He apparently remembered the day on Grass Mountain and turned to nod at her with a smile.

"It's been a long time. I've been meaning to thank you for the tea that day. I've been drafted, and I may not return. If something happens to me, will you promise to burn a stick of incense for me?"

He finished with a sad smile. She was flustered, and before she could think of something proper in response, he said expansively,

"So long!"

He left with other draftees. What happened to him later? He might have died in battle. But if he did make it back, who knew where he was now? Like a flower on a peak, unreachable.

Her sentimental recollection of the college student brought back one scene after another from those days, but the memories produced only loneliness and dissatisfaction, making her feel even more lost, like living alone on a mountain, beset by unbearable loneliness and bone-chilling bleakness. A few days earlier, she'd felt the same sort of boredom and, unable to stay calmly at home, had roamed the streets for a long time. But in the end, she'd failed to quiet her chaotic thoughts, while emptiness grew inside.

She was in a similar emotional state when Fan stopped by.

"How are you, Miss Yulan?" he greeted her while opening the package.

"Just a little something. I'd be pleased if you'd accept it."

She froze when he handed it to her. It was an expensive, colorful handbag that brightened up everything around them.

The costly gift alarmed her. She declined over and over, but ended up taking it because he said he could not return it to the store.

The one she'd really wanted to meet had not shown up, while she'd run into so many she didn't care to know. Now all this belonged to the past, since in the end, no one with true feelings for her was anywhere to be found. Then, when she was lonely and bored, awaiting the man of her dreams, Fan Hanzhi had appeared, and she was drawn to him unconsciously, like a sunflower to the sun.

"Zhaofeng Park must be really nice, Mr. Fan. I'd love to visit it."

Captivated by Fan's descriptions, she dreamed of going to Shanghai to see the much-touted department stores, dance halls, movie theaters that showed foreign films, and parks. To her, Taipei seemed so rural, with nothing worthy of note. Their conversation progressed from the parks in Shanghai to the scenery in Beitou and Grass Mountain, and Fan suggested that they take a trip together. Her young heart was gripped by the need to go out of the city for spring sightseeing.

The car drove out of the disorderly lanes and onto Zhongshan North Road, where it was smooth sailing. A gentle breeze sent fresh air into her heart.

Roadside trees had just put on a new coat of green. Yulan was enthralled by Datun shan, standing majestically amid distant clouds, a display of boundless masculine strength and beauty. Spring had also made an appearance on the greening Yuan shan nearby. The car was soon driving alongside the Keelung River after crossing Zhongshan Bridge.

"How's my driving—ha-ha?" He turned to say. "The newspapers have been attacking people who use government vehicles for their private use. This, however, is my own car."

The words emerging between his white teeth betrayed his self-satisfaction. He had been unhappy with Shanghai women, who were only modern on the surface. He found Yulan's refreshing manner enchanting, like an urbanite tiring of stale fruit tasting fresh oranges in an orchard. They followed the rail line onto a mountain road after leaving Shilin behind. Peach trees were blooming all along the way, enveloping them in a world of flowers. With their car encircled by mist, and flowers greeting them, they felt somewhat giddy, as if visiting a dream world; Yulan was finally getting a taste of spring, something she'd nearly missed. Sweet talk pushed the scene out of her mind, however, while the pretty flowers helped remove all her worries. Wandering like a sleepwalker inspired by the mysterious Datun shan, she felt herself melting away in the heart of Nature. The car continued down the road, eventually stopping in front of a bathhouse.

It was Sunday, but the place had few visitors. They checked into a room, small, but with a vase of flowers that brought spring into the space. It was completely different from the time she'd come with her friends. She went into the bathing room quietly and sank into the water to let it wash away all her worries. Her nicely proportioned body spread out freely; gazing at her own fair, ample limbs bobbing in the milky white water, she had to admit that she was quite lovely. "If at this moment he . . ."

She caught herself and blushed out of shame, even though she was among female bathers. No one knew her thoughts, of course, but she nonetheless hastily came out of the water, got dressed, and went back to the room.

Fan had not returned from the men's bath, so she sat down at the window to cool off with her private thoughts. It was a quiet, secluded room, with bird songs being the only sound she could hear, too serene even for a cat.

Though this was not her first visit to Grass Mountain, she could not have imagined a place like this even in her dreams. It suddenly occurred to her that this might not be the kind of place for her, a thought that undermined her composure. Soon Fan came back and her disquiet lessened, only to be replaced by the unease of being alone with a man. She felt she was doing something wrong, and her conscience reproached her, but just as she wondered if she should go home, a waiter brought in their lunch.

The sun had tilted to the West when they walked out of the bathhouse and strolled to the clubhouse. Under the caress of a gentle breeze, Yulan felt her thoughts running wild now that she had shed her post-bath lethargy. Butterflies with white and yellow patterns chased each other among the flowers, as young couples walked around them. Birds were singing, flowers were competing to be the prettiest, and the world was brimming with the feel of spring. A stream gurgled down a narrow glen like skittering pieces of jade. Listening to sweet talk from Fan and savoring the beautiful sights before her, Yulan almost wished they could go on walking forever. They reached the clubhouse, whose front was also decorated with flowers in full bloom, against a ground paved with fine grains of pure white sand.

A young couple walked toward them holding hands. When they got closer, Yulan stopped short; the world is never too big for coincidences. The woman, Miss Huiying, was a fellow member of the Gull Society (an organization created by the Japanese during World War II to recruit recent female high school graduates to serve as special nurses). Fan realized the young man was a good friend of his, Chen Deqing, whom Fan had not seen for several years. They had both been part of the Northern Expedition but had lost touch during the war with Japan. It appeared that Chen had come to Taiwan from Chongqing, an uncomfortable reference to Fan, who had worked for the puppet government in Shanghai. He greeted his old friend with a hint of a guilty conscience and, as they related what they'd been up to since their last time together, a happy smile emerged on his face over their chance encounter after all these years.

Huiying and Yulan, as members of the society, had been sent to Hong Kong together as special nurses; upon their return, Huiying had been promoted to be an administrator, for she was undauntingly active. She joined the special squad of the Kominka Hokokai and could often be seen on stage giving impassioned speeches to the public, whether it was a send-off for the soldiers, condolence visits with family members of the dead, injured, and sick soldiers, or donation collecting, and so on. It was truly a golden age for her, for she was considered a representative of all Taiwanese women, and her name frequently appeared in print. But her mentality had changed in the new era. She had gone every morning to pray at a Japanese shrine, but now the altar had been removed and replaced with a picture of Dr. Sun Yat-sen. She'd also shed her Japanese clothes at some point and put on expensive qipaos, the so-called post-retrocession posture. A Chinese officer took the place of Japanese soldiers walking with her.

"Miss Yulan, you too . . ."

They shook hands, covering up things with a smile, and then parted after a brief introduction of their respective male friends.

Yulan and Fan walked around the clubhouse, through a tunnel of foliage, and into the hills. With no one in sight, it was quiet, an occasional falling leaf disturbing the silence. She was visited by an unknown emotion, her heart racing as if a fawn were running in her chest. Fan walked up and wrapped his arms around her from behind. She recoiled but could not shake him off despite her repeated attempts. Something heavy pressed down on her, while blood pulsated through her body; she could almost hear her own heartbeat. In the end, she gave up and fell into his arms, entranced, as if in a dream.

A noise came from somewhere; his hands fell away and he eased the hold on her. It was a bird flapping its wings.

Somehow, they found themselves off to the side of the clubhouse, which was deadly quiet inside. Its grandeur gone, the clubhouse grounds were covered with fallen petals.

New bathers appeared to be arriving. They returned to the bathhouse in high spirits.

On their way back to the city, they made a detour to Beitou, following the hillside path by Shamao shan. To their left was a small flat area at the foothills with lush green fields. An expanse of emerald green waves extended beyond the Tamsui River toward the ocean. On the far river bank, Guanyin shan stood in the glow of a setting sun, under which a train leaving Tamsui, like a row of match boxes, skimmed through a spring scene that spread as far as the eye could see. A breeze blew in through the car window and cooled her face while she lost herself in the changing spring scenes. It felt somewhat bittersweet. Suddenly Fan turned and smiled. Instinctively, she smiled back. The downhill drive went fast, and soon they'd left Upper Beitou and reached Beitou proper, from where they followed the rail line and sailed through the town as if gliding across water. She was so enthralled she didn't even notice Hell Valley along the way, as she chased after the illusion of spring.

5

A black curtain had descended quietly on earth when Yulan went out on the street, dressed in a newly tailored Shanghai-style qipao and carrying the purse from Fan. Likely because she hadn't worn qipaos often enough, the hem kept getting in the way and made it hard for her to walk. Her fancy dress and purse were eye-catching, so she avoided busy streets, not wanting to run into anyone she knew. Quietly, she turned from a three-lane road over to a park at an intersection. The bomb craters had been filled in unevenly with broken tiles and bricks, ideal ground for weeds. Air raid shelters, no longer in use, looked dark and deep. Keeping her eyes down, she walked up to a streetlight by a tree to wait. When a crowd swarmed over from Wenwu Street, she studied them intently. A glance at her watch told her she was too early, so she opened her purse out of boredom. Her hand mirror shone brightly even at night. She wanted to check her makeup, but the light was too weak. She grew impatient, not knowing what to do next.

Fan Hanzhi felt ten years younger after the trip to Grass Mountain. A life without romance condemned one to living in an overwrought state, ending up running around like a wild dog. Seen this way, romantic love was not a luxury or an extravagance. No, one should say that anyone with no time for love either suffered from a nervous disorder, was rabidly materialistic, or was power hungry. Rising above fame and wealth to love was the apex of beautiful poetry.

Half a lifetime's hard work and effort had vanished, leaving nothing behind but pervasive darkness and hypocrisy, for which he could never completely account. As a result, for him, everything had been a means to an end. After losing hope in life, he was left with only material gains and sexual gratification. In China, in particular, money was omnipotent, and even romantic love was compensation for money. When he first met Yulan, it had been a brief dalliance, the pursuit of an amusement. But at some point, he'd grown attached to her. Her virginal frankness and innocence, something he'd never encountered in China, had touched him deeply, to the point that, since their first meeting, he'd been out of sorts as he waited for Sundays to arrive. To relieve his loneliness, he'd asked Yulan out for a stroll. He left his lodging way before the prearranged time, telling himself that she wouldn't come out so easily, and decided he'd go straight to her house if she didn't show. With his mind plagued by such thoughts, he quickened his steps and reached the park, where he spotted her standing under a tree.

He raced up. She gave him the hint of a bashful smile before casting her eyes down.

"Shall we go, Miss Yulan?"

She went with him, happy to be walking with a man who was interested in her. And yet she was shy and somewhat fearful, her heart beating so fast she couldn't compose herself. Her eyes took in everything, but they left no impression. All she saw was a blur.

Even if her parents were to appear, they might as well be strangers.

She followed him to a dance hall. There were no hired dance girls, but many young Japanese women. As the music played through the speakers, they started dancing, with teachers or with each other. Fan took the lead. Yulan had studied dance in high school, so to her social dancing came rather easily, and she was moving nicely after learning a few basic steps. Since it was still a bit new, she was too focused on her feet to fully enjoy herself, like most everyone else. Still, she danced away, her blood surging through her, until she was bathed in dream-like sweat. The pleasure was a brand-new sensation. During a break, she took a deep breath when a cold wind blew in over her feverish face through the blinds. The evening wind was refreshing and energizing. They danced late into the spring night until the sky was a fish-belly white. Her young blood was at the height of excitement.

Doing something new for the first time is hard, but not the second time; one should always try a second tasting of a delicacy, after which you are addicted. That was true for Yulan. She had started out timidly, but after a few visits, she was like an opium smoker and went out with Fan every night.

One night, after coming out of the dance hall, they strolled along deserted streets and soon walked past the National Theater, where the area, devoid of streetlights, was shrouded in darkness and endless silence. Fan moved closer to her. It was late, and the doors of houses along the streets were shut, with only faint glows seeping through. Their feet made a soft rustling noise on the fine sand, when he suddenly put his arm around her. It was the same arm, but it felt different from earlier at the dance hall, for she could sense his flesh through her clothes. No, it was the blood roaring in his veins pounding on her heart. She stopped, unconsciously, to savor the intoxicating embrace.

She felt his soft lips at the same time, the first in her life, a privilege to a virgin. Blood raced through her body and her heart thudded madly. Ah, so this is what a man . . .

"I love you, Miss Yulan."

His voice was like music drifting down from heaven.

"Ah, this must be what they mean by the spring of one's life."

They embraced silently until they realized they were near the Tamsui River, where people appeared to be milling about. They started walking again, both rendered wordless by the exhilaration they'd shared. When they got to the third sluice gate, they saw a couple cooing to each other, but quickly walked off when they drew closer. Fan sat down on a stone piling at the dock. Like willow catkins tossed by the wind, she fell weakly into his lap, and they repeated their earlier tender moments. She was in a trance, hearing nothing but his rapid breathing.

"Will you marry me, Miss Yulan?"

She hesitated, unsure how to respond, when his soft lips pressed down on her and brought her immense bliss.

Ah! Spring, spring time. On this spring night.

Oh, every minute of a spring night is priceless.

The water flowed silently in the river. It must have been very late, for all was quiet. The lights on the distant Taipei Bridge had a hazy glow, outlining the charming shape of Guanyin shan. Something, maybe a fisherman's boat, glided across the river, trailed by light yellow glints on the water's surface.

6

Huiying and her new husband came to visit shortly after their wedding. The groom was in an army uniform, with a pistol and ammunition on his belt. Children who had never seen an armed man fled into their houses when they saw him. Yulan's mother came out to greet them with a bit of trepidation. Yulan wasn't surprised, since she'd met them on Grass Mountain. Giving her friend heartfelt good wishes, she thought of a similar future for herself. After Huiying left, residents in the neighborhood talked about marrying a man from China. Yulan's mother thought of Huiying as a smart girl, for she had been the head of the Gull Society. When everything had been scarce during the war, she'd had no trouble buying items in the Army Shop that were unavailable on the black market, things like rationed meat, oil, towels, and soap, items that even money couldn't buy.

"When the Japanese came," an older man said, "some of the hooligans in Dadaocheng went to greet them and were rewarded with official titles."

"Ai-ya, so what! Some people had it easier than that. The son of a cook for an army officer got a position befitting a colonel because he knew a few Japanese words."

Yulan's father told everyone the story he'd heard from their neighborhood chief. At a time like this, it was advantageous to be associated with anyone from China, which was a shared view. Yulan was secretly happy to hear that.

"Right," she told herself, "don't wait any longer. Tonight . . ."

She went to her mother's room after dinner. Luckily her father was out, or she would not have known how to broach the subject.

"Ma."

Her mother paused in her needlework when she heard Yulan and looked up. Yulan still could not bring herself to talk about it.

"What's the matter, Yulan?" her mother asked tenderly.

"Ma, he and I . . ." She lowered her head, blushing to her earlobes.

"You and Mr. Fan?" Her mother tilted her head.

"Yes."

"Are you going to marry him?"

Yulan merely nodded with a subtle squirm of her shoulders, grateful for her mother's understanding. Fan had been coming to their house every day. Age was not an issue, and Mother would not object. Father would likely give his consent too, especially since girls' marriages had been delayed by the war, and soon after the retrocession, they married, one after another, like butterflies in late spring. And not just Taiwanese, but Japanese too. Under such circumstances, Yulan's marriage would encounter no objections. By the end of the month, their names were published in the advertisement section of the local paper and, from that day on, Yulan was Mrs. Fan, a newly minted housewife. The taste of romance was as sweet as Coca Cola. But marriage is a mixture of salty, sour, sweet, and spicy flavors.

Being a section chief, Fan Hanzhi was able to take over a large house that had belonged to a Japanese. Fierce fights were breaking out over the seizure of Japanese property, some between government officials, some between government officials and ordinary people, some among the people themselves. It happened just about every day. Hired thugs carried out sham transactions by colluding with soldiers or Japanese. By hook or by crook, anyone who was someone searched for Japanese property like a hawk.

On the second day of Yulan's new life, she heard gunfire in the middle of the night. Like a thunderclap in a clear sky, it woke her from a sweet dream and worried her.

The sound of rapid footsteps receded, and the night returned to silence. Putting her hand on her racing heart, Yulan could not figure out what might have happened. The night deepened. All of a sudden, she felt her husband drift away from her, so she turned to check; he was fast asleep under a down blanket.

Beginning to tremble from a sudden sense of loneliness, she slid over to be near him. Reflexively, he reached out and gently put his arm around her, removing her fear. She felt like a chick protected by its mother after a hawk attack.

The next morning, she heard neighbors clamoring outside. She wanted to go out and take a look, but she didn't because of her status as a new bride; she would be visiting her parents on the third day after the wedding. They sent someone to bring her home around nine. The escort and her parents all knew what had happened the night before, but they were too frightened to talk about it. As she walked out the door, Yulan saw a young man lying in the ditch across the way, and that told her what the previous night's gunfire meant. He looked like a student. A child, standing beside the body, was being questioned by passersby. She couldn't help hearing that the young man was killed over the seizure of Japanese property. Sitting in the rickshaw on her way home, she reflected on the turmoil that was destroying society. She hadn't gotten a good look at the young man's face, but he did seem familiar. Could it have been the college student she'd met on Grass Mountain? Faces of people, from childhood friends to young men she knew, flashed before her. She shut her eyes and continued to scroll through scenes. A bugle blared, and Japanese soldiers gathered like swarming ants on the spacious athletic field, spirited, ready to go to war. She had joined them as a nurse, considering it the greatest honor. The sky was high and the water clear; Japanese fleets pressed forward in the South China Sea and reached Hong Kong, where Chinese lay dead on the streets and in the ditches. She hadn't had any strong feelings at the time. Those were her compatriots, but now people in Taiwan . . . .. The rickshaw rocked as it came to a stop outside her parents' house. Her mother came out, her siblings greeted her with broad smiles, so she too walked in with a smile, holding her husband's hand.

7

On a warm spring day, Fan Hanzhi took his wife on a honeymoon trip. Riding in a second-class compartment immediately elevated Yulan's status. The train whistled as it left Taipei on its southward journey. Sitting in the cushioned seat, she exchanged sweet nothings with Fan, with her eyes on the scenery outside. Everywhere she looked lush green signs of spring were visible in the fields, mountains, and rivers. After leaving the Banqiao station, she could see on the right, off in the distance, Guanyin shan lay under a blue sky. It looked as if it had taken in too much air, for its "chest" was puffed up, which made the "nose" seem squat. Gazing at the lovely mountain, Yulan jerked her head around when she heard him blowing his nose with his fingers. She frowned, but he did not notice and continued making a honking noise. That grated on her nerves. If it had been a child, she'd have corrected him, but she couldn't tell her husband in public to stop doing that. She had to suppress her disgust and sigh privately while turning to gaze out the window again.

The train picked up speed after passing Taoyuan and began to sway as it sped through a long, narrow valley onto a broad expanse of flatland. The emerald green fields extended to the horizon and merged with the ocean under a clear blue sky. It filled her with enormous joy to see towering whistling pines sway in the breeze and water buffaloes amble among them.

The sight reminded her of a day in her childhood on her grandmother's birthday. She and her mother encountered a similarly serene countryside, where verdant fields were dotted with egrets; in the breeze, the whistling pines murmured like a stream. A buffalo, with big, thick horns, shuffled its hefty body, frightening her when it got closer. Its malodorous droppings were unbearable; flies dispersed when it swished its tail but soon gathered around it again. When it walked by, a boy about her age hollered at the animal and hit it with a bamboo switch. The buffalo jumped in fright, snorting heavily and shaking its head, its large eyes glaring at them.

Yulan shrieked and pressed herself against her mother. Her heart stirred at the memory.

"What are you thinking about, Yulan?" Fan asked.

She mumbled a reply but kept her eyes on the scene beyond the window. When he laid his hand gently on her shoulder, she shook it reflexively, almost imperceptibly. It was their honeymoon trip, an enjoyable event, but she was lonely and felt that something was missing, the emotion of someone who realized that what she'd gotten wasn't quite what she'd wanted. Recollections of happy days only managed to dilute her beautiful illusion with a hint of sorrow. After roaring over several steel bridges, the train reached Xinzhu, where the station had nearly been demolished by bombings; she could still feel the terror of war. Nothing was left of the sturdy steel-and-cement structure, which wore on her frayed nerves and reminded her of a series of wartime events. She'd been working at the Mackay Hospital in Gongqianding. The hospital belonged to a neutral country and wasn't near any major targets, not Songshan Airport, the Taipei Train Station, or Taipei Bridge, which everyone was sure would be bombed. Moreover, the American Consulate and a church with a soaring spire that could be easily spotted were in the vicinity. She'd thought the area near the hospital was safe, but it had been destroyed in an air strike on the first of October.

It had also been a clear day, with only puffy white clouds resting atop Datun shan. The autumn sun had lost its intensity, though it was still hot outside. At the bus kiosk by the intersection the usual dozens of riders waited for a bus. Suddenly, sirens blared, an eerie, bleak sound that made everyone's heart skip a beat; they were like lambs led to the slaughter, waiting for fate to dole out life or death, while the pilots held the power in their hands. In the blink of an eye, they took the lives of even the kindest people. It made no difference whether they were gentlemen, philosophers, moralists, philanthropists, wartime pleasure seekers, or power mongers, for they were all sentenced to death without a trial and executed in the cruelest manner possible.

"When did Heaven give them the authority to kill?"

Anger rose as she reached this point in her thoughts, when she spotted patients stumbling into an air raid shelter, while those who could not walk were being carried in on stretchers by nurses. Yulan, with all those thoughts on her mind, was late getting in. The sound of propeller blades was getting louder, coming toward her from the north, and, before she knew it, a Grumman aircraft flew over her head. She threw herself in as a rattling, explosion nearly deafened her. Dust and smoke rose into the air; she was shaking uncontrollably from the terror, even her teeth were clattering. Shrieking noises were followed by those of collapsing buildings, quaking earth, and explosions. Speechless now, she was rooted to the spot, dumbfounded. More noise came, when a bomb landed on a nearby shelter, ripping off arms and legs, trailed by the heavy smell of sulfur. It took eight lives—two doctors, three nurses, and three patients. All the windows in the building were shattered, glass shards lay strewn atop sick beds. Yulan could still see the ashen faces of the nurses, one who was missing part of her leg, and covered in blood, breathing laboriously, her pale lips quivering as she was carried into an operating room that was half blown away. Two or three assistants were needed to pin her down to have her leg amputated without anesthesia. Her groans lingered in Yulan's ears. At the time if it had been . . . fear gripped her as she thought about it even now. She knew she was extremely lucky to have escaped such a horrible fate.

The door to their car clanged open and interrupted her wild thoughts. Several passengers came to sit behind them, and silence returned. As the train left Xinzhu station, she could hear what those behind her were saying.

"Girls are nothing but trouble in wartime, like unsellable radishes that rot quickly and are aggressively forced onto all kinds of people."

"Don't be so put out. It's all because our Taiwanese men have foolish sentiments but no ambition. They attempt nothing and accomplish nothing, and yet they're arrogant and conceited, so no young women would chase after them, no matter where they went."

"What do you mean? That's insulting. I've been all over the world."

"You see? Boasting again. No wonder young women don't like you."

"It's not our young men's fault, it's women who can be had for a bargain. I heard about a company or a bank, I don't remember which, anyhow, there were many wartime girls, all in their late twenties, and all looking for a mate. Then a super modish young man arrived from Shanghai. He wore a double-breasted suit, wide-rimmed glasses, a showy tie, a fancy belt, and a gold watch. His hair was slicked down so smoothly a fly would stick to it. Those women, who'd seen nothing but old, soiled suits and muddy shoes, were stunned into staring dumbly. But you can never trust a man who cares that much about how he looks. He was all smiles when he proposed to every woman who flirted with him, and before a month was over, he had eight fiancées. No matter how talented he was, he didn't know which one to keep."

Yulan was annoyed, for it sounded like they were talking about her. They lowered their voices so she couldn't hear what they were saying any longer, but they kept erupting into obnoxious laughter. No matter how she tried to ignore them, she assumed they were criticizing her. Then one of them raised his voice again, seemingly on purpose,

"I heard about something bizarre that happened down south. An old maid somehow met a modish man from the Motherland. His clothes were so fancy her father thought he must be a high official. The man knew how to toot his own horn too. She wasn't the only one who fell under his spell; her whole family was taken by him. Her parents accepted his marriage proposal. He presented them with twenty thousand dollars, on top of other betrothal gifts, a gold watch, gold bracelets, gold rings, and so on. The country bumpkins were duly impressed, of course. Their relatives and their neighbors were green with envy. The greedy ones among them believed they'd reap tremendous benefits from marrying a mainland Chinese, like back when the Japanese took over Taiwan. When the Japanese invaded Taiwan, the ones who carried briefcases for Japanese officers were given official titles, so no wonder the country folks were envious. The woman strutted around, mightily pleased, as if she were already married. But it all fell apart the day after the wedding. Turns out, the large sum of money had been pooled together by four men. So, she wasn't the wife or the mistress of a single man. She was just . . . her sweet dream was shattered, and there'd be no official titles, of course."

The man laughed when he finished. But what he said was exactly the same as the comments made by Yulan's parents when her friend, Huiying, came to visit right after her wedding. Yulan was terribly upset. The men couldn't be mocking her because they knew her parents' worries, could they? Whether a woman got married or not was often subject to people's gossip, and that annoyed her. But she had to put up with it despite her unhappiness. The train had reached an open coastal area, where the waves crashing against the shore gave off a white light. The horizon was filled with whitecaps on the ocean surface, and puffy white clouds skimmed across the clear sky. A honeymoon in a person's limited time on earth was supposed to bring limitless pleasure, but unfortunately there were the two chatterboxes spewing unpleasant talk. Peeved, she moved up to a seat in front.

For a moment she was free to take in the scenery, a carefree ocean coast reflecting the gentle spring sunshine, tiny ripples spreading across the water, and white sails gliding with the wind. Fatigue stole up on her after a while. Nights for newlyweds tend to pass quickly, and dawn came all too soon, before she was well rested. She'd wanted to continue their intimate moments, but soon it was twelve o'clock, then one, then two. Now after three hours on the rocking train, she dozed off as the train continued traveling south along the smooth coastline.

They were at Ershui station when she was roused from her dreams, and the scenery outside, replete with southern flavor, was drastically different. Farmhouses under carefree betel nut palms were encircled by bamboo groves, behind which lay rounded hills covered in green. The bamboo groves had a pale-yellow tint that caught her eye as the tall bamboo swayed elegantly in the wind to show off the flair of a southern farm village, a mix of green, yellow, and purple shades. Betel nut palms, banana shrubs, and papaya trees proudly decorated the areas around the houses, like a refreshing simple painting. As she enjoyed the serene sight, a poetic experience, they got off to switch to the Jiji line.

Beggars in tattered clothes swarmed the station, women with children on their backs, blind old women, pale young men, all imploring with pitiful voices. Yulan gave each some money when suddenly someone thrust a hand up to her wordlessly. It was a bloodless hand, icy cold and ghastly pale. Yulan was so spooked she took a step back. A filthy woman stared wildly and silently at her, dribble hanging from the corner of her mouth. It was such a sad sight that Yulan hurriedly took some money from her purse and tossed it to the woman before walking out onto the platform, where a child covered in dirt was selling peanuts. Not a big deal, but the sight annoyed her.

Soon the train for Shuilikeng pulled into the station. It was a rickety train, with no first- or second-class seats, only third class. The car's interior was like an open market, with children hawking their wares: cookies, cornstarch jelly, patent medicines, sticky rice and pork wrapped in bamboo leaves, and peanuts. They crowded onto the cars to make sales. A great many bundles, including rice, vegetables, and chickens, were brought onto the car at every stop. At Zhuoshui station, a man carrying baskets of ducks tried to squeeze in through a window, filling the car with the ducks' quacks and stench. Those by the window tried to stop him, but he ignored them and pushed his flock in, forcing the people nearby to stand up and let the ducks in. The vendor followed them in through the window, to everyone's displeasure. Passengers who were soiled in the process got into a row with the vendor but could do nothing about it. Everyone wore a scornful look and one passenger mocked,

"Domestic animals have raised their status since the retrocession. Now chickens and ducks can ride on trains too."

"Freedom and equality for pigs and ducks," a neatly dressed man next to him joined in. "What can we do about it?"

That made everyone laugh, but not Yulan, who had a feeling that they were in fact criticizing her husband, transferring their feelings about the Japanese onto anyone from China. People had welcomed them with open arms shortly after the retrocession, but six months had barely passed when the sentiments were replaced by unhappy, angry looks. They even gave her a disdainful glare.

In groups of four or five, the children pushed their way into a car that did not have any standing room, hawking peanuts or sticky rice with pork. The passengers told them there was no room, but they didn't care and kept pushing to the point that many riders were lifted off their feet. Yulan was one of them. When her feet finally came back down, someone stepped on her shoe.

"Ouch!" She pushed the man away. Her beautiful Shanghai shoe was all muddy, the first disaster since her wedding. She was mightily put out, and a thought occurred to her: our people should not behave this way.

The thought unsettled her. The train began laboring up a hill, with her hemmed in on all sides, unable to move. She wished they could get off, but she had to suffer another half hour before they reached Shuilikeng. It was a small jumble of a station. Rough-looking manual laborers got off the train. The couple took a bus to Sun Moon Lake, not arriving till dusk. If they had taken their own car, they'd have been able to enjoy the scenery along the way, but in the crowded bus she saw nothing but hills and trees on both sides, a very common view. The lake scenery, on the other hand, was out of this world. On a hill over seven hundred meters above sea level, water from time immemorial, ancient and dark green, almost frighteningly green, sparkled with a mysterious emerald hue. Hills were reflected in the vast lake with a calm mirror-like surface, where canoes moved gracefully. The scenery called up visions from thousands of years before. Before customs arising from civilization took root here, naked men and women danced and sang with their wooden clubs, sharing private moments on canoes or singing under a bright moon, living out their lives in nature. With no worries caused by civilization, no one hungered for money or power, and no despicable materialists ever existed among them. They had no need to compete with each other; instead, they slept among flowers, sang on the lake. They danced drunkenly under cherry blossoms in the spring, listened to gurgling streams in the summer, gazed at the moon with a loved one in the fall, and appreciated the snow in the winter, awaiting the arrival of spring. Deeply inspired by the mystery of nature, Yulan longed for the ancient times as she walked hand in hand with Fan along the lakeshore.

The paved winding path was swept clean; cherry trees on both sides were just sprouting. A gentle breeze caressed her breasts, and young blood she'd forgotten about for years surged in her; she felt as if she'd returned to her youth. Listening to birds singing on treetops, she looked at the placid water and thought about earlier times, with dancing indigenous tribes and the rhythmic pounding sound of their wooden clubs. They were worry-free and carefree, no rules of etiquette to follow, no law to turn someone into a slave. How she longed for an unaffected, unfettered society like that.

As her thoughts wandered, they reached Hanbi Villa, a Japanese structure offering clean rooms, quiet and spacious, with a view of the lake as well as the Shuishe Mountains across the shore. White clouds hung above the mountaintops, against the colorful glow of the setting sun, a wondrous sight completely different from what one saw down below. It grew dark quickly, as the sun set and brought a chill into the air. She would recover her vitality after spending a night by the splendid lake.

The sun rises late in the mountains. Tired from the trip, she slept in and woke up around nine-thirty. Unlike down below, up here the morning was cool. After breakfast, she sat across from Fan in a rattan chair to gaze at the lake. It was so tranquil. White clouds, gossamer-like, drifting overhead, seemed cottony soft. No clamor or any kind of noise. She felt her whole person merging with nature. It would be wonderful if she could sit there forever, she thought, when she noticed Fan take out a notebook to write something. He read what he'd written before handing it to her.

> Hill beyond hill, lake behind lake,
> Deep in the white clouds, a single orb.
> Water flows in serene Sun Moon Lake,
> a canoe carries a carefree fisherman.
>
> Unrestrained songs, wooden club music, exquisite as jade,
> Autumn water and the sky become one.
> Admiring the sun and moon at Hanbi Villa,
> Hills are reflected in the lake.

It was a poem about the lake, which she didn't understand completely, despite the self-satisfied look on his face. After reciting it loudly, he sang it softly, but he couldn't sit quietly any longer, so he began to pace the room as he sang. That went on for a while before he invited her to visit the indigenous tribe at Shuishe.

They took a canoe. With homespun cloth draped over his shoulders, their boatman sang as he paddled along. It was pure joy to sail across the ancient, timeless waters of the vast lake surrounded by the serene mountains. She was captivated, especially by the deep blue water that seemed to transmit something mysterious to her. The canoe glided silently across a lake that was over a hundred feet deep, which gave the water a rich hue, seemingly deeper than the ocean. She felt she could enjoy the happiness of a newlywed once again. It would not be easy for a single woman, no matter how rich, to come here, and even if she made it, she might not necessarily have such a soothing, relaxing experience.

"It's good to have a man, after all," she said to herself.

The canoe moved slowly, creating tiny ripples as it went. She was too absorbed by the scenery to realize they'd arrived at Shuishe. It was a small village by the lake, most of its indigenous flavor gone, for hints of civilization had adulterated its primitive colors. The mystery of ancient nature was being corroded by destructive artificiality. Such a pity. But as she watched the dance and listened to their pounding clubs, her soul was seemingly lured into a secluded spot in the mountain, away from reality. She traveled, in spirit, to a preternatural realm, where she danced freely. Nature's mystery turned into the clubs beating out delightful rhythms, while the performers sang as a group along with the light melody, emitting a sweet, clear sound to rend the silence in the mountain. She was lost, drunken, in this wondrous world. In nature, she forgot herself and her husband, her thoughts roaming back in time to imagine a myriad world and experience something she'd never had in the city— the true value of nature manifested in simple smiles.

The sun shone the next day as they left the mountain and headed to Tainan, where they visited Koxinga's Temple, the Tomb of the Five Consorts, and Chikan Tower. Everywhere they went they saw footprints of the Dutch from three hundred years earlier, when they settled in the savage land and built a city. Later, Koxinga consolidated and expanded the Dutch development, also leaving behind relics. Against such an ancient backdrop, the Persian silk trees planted by the Japanese appeared exceptionally graceful. She knew nothing about the worrisome spring of the south under the silk trees, but she found herself getting sentimental. Road repairs had yet to be completed, so they skipped Anping and set out for Kaohsiung.

Kaohsiung was still in ruins, a picture of hell from the ravages of war, steel and concrete rubble littering the street. She couldn't imagine how a modern city that had taken fifty years to build could suffer that degree of damage. Buildings housing the county office and city hall had been totally bombed out. She cried out despite herself, Oh, my! Why did you have to give people knowledge? She couldn't stop blaming the heavens, as sad tears rolled down her face. This had once been the southern base of Japanese Imperialism, with the best of science behind its modernization project, but nothing had come of it. Now the Japanese Empire's ambition had been thwarted, leaving behind only this frightening sight.

> Ah! Kaohsiung. Kaohsiung.
> Since the beginning of history,
> you should have been allowed to grow naturally
> and get old naturally.
> Despicable humans,
> because of their greedy desire,
> turned you into a battlefield,
> changing your beauty with blood and flesh.
> Ai! tens of thousands of our people
> wept bitter tears over you.

She was aggrieved to see her people, fatigued from sobbing, gasping for air as they struggled. Wherever they went in the city, the sad sight of war assaulted her nerves. She saw nothing but desolation, the carnage of war glaring everywhere in the sun, broken bricks and shattered tiles strewn across the ground, tadpoles swimming in pools created by bomb craters. She shuddered at the aftermath of a cruel war. They strolled around and soon she was weary, physically and mentally. To give her frayed nerves some respite, she headed toward Shou shan, but it was overgrown with weeds, its former appearance gone. Standing atop to gaze into distance still presented a pleasant vista, however. Inside the harbor were several blasted ships that had run aground, their hulls half submerged, only the masts still standing, but not for long. She looked at the promontory at Hongmao Harbor, where the waves from Bashi Channel lapped against the shore, raising sprays of foam before receding to meet with the boundless green waves and returning to the sea; the horizon was a white line formed by gentle ripples and the blue sky. Far off on the water an ocean liner sailed leisurely. She felt she could gaze at the scene forever, as her mood was brightened by the expanse of green waves. Fan spoke up out of the blue,

"This isn't much fun, Yulan. Let's go back." There was no harshness in his comment, and she sensed how he felt, so she walked down the hill with him despite her displeasure in having to leave.

8

Being in love before marriage had the flavor of yogurt, while the honeymoon trip tasted like oranges, which was what Yulan felt as she experienced several days of slight tartness and a sweetness that was just right. It was unforgettable, though riding on trains and walking around every day was tiring. But she was still a new bride, so she continued to seek pleasure after their return.

Soon summer arrived. She was still tired, likely because of the trip, so one day she spread out the bedding to lie down after her husband left for work. It was a quiet morning, and she hoped to have a good nap but could not sleep. Nestled in the soft bed, she could not stop all sorts of thoughts from bubbling up. In a seemingly drunken, stupefied state, she called to mind every detail of her new life, her mind intent upon bringing back everything; she nearly succeeded. One experienced pleasure mixed with exasperation while in pursuit of something, but what one obtained seemed to pale greatly in comparison with what one failed to reach, and that led to dissatisfaction. No, it was more like a bird that is lovelier soaring in the sky than in a cage. It was a contradiction she experienced often. Back in high school, she'd thought the cut flowers at a friend's house were lovely, so she asked for some and brought them back to put in her living room. Barely a few hours later, she was tired of them and took them back to her friend. And this wasn't the only time. She'd wanted a cicada since childhood, but once she got one, she found it boring and stomped it to death. On summer evenings when it began to cool off, the rosy glow of a sunset painted the sky red. A cicada's drawn-out, quivering song cut through the quiet dusk, as if pouring its heart out to a potential mate; it sounded romantic. Then another one, on a different branch, would sing as if in response. Boundless beauty exuded from their sweet melody in the fading light of the evening. When one stopped, the other began to sing, like murmuring lovers among humans, but more bewitching. She could not stop wanting to catch one when she heard them. Once, over summer break after her first year in high school, she caught one with a friend, but it refused to make the same kind of pretty sound; instead it just shrieked annoyingly, no matter what she did. It kept shrieking until she lost her temper, threw it to the ground, and stomped it to death. Without trying, she recalled these incidents. Summer was indeed here, when she noticed for the first time the lush, dark green trees in the yard. Where would she go to enjoy the cicada singing this year? She couldn't think of a place.

It was quiet; the maid must have gone out. Yulan quietly got out of bed. The house was replete with Japanese flavor: the furniture—wardrobe, mirrored dressing table—and paintings in the living room, all seized from the Japanese. The furnishings were a perfect match for the Chinese juniper floor, which she liked very much. When she thought about it, she was surprised that her husband could so effortlessly take control of such a grand and well-appointed Japanese house, especially at a time when disputes over seizure occurred almost daily. She had to admire his ability to get his hands on so much Japanese property. He'd said the Japanese are a docile people; when he told the man to leave the wardrobe, he obliged, the same with the mirrored dressing table, without protest. The fearful wolves had turned into timid lambs, a change that perplexed her. Why would they submit to Mainland Chinese so easily? It was beyond her imagination when she recalled how the Japanese had treated the Taiwanese. But why would her husband take their property for nothing? She was mortified by his shameless act, and found the furnishings both despicable and embarrassing, worse than how he left his shoes in the alcove. Sometimes, he even forgot to take them off and walked on the tatami like a chicken. His behavior reminded her of an uncultured man with inferior upbringing. Now that she was spending so much time alone in a big house, these incidents popped into her head frequently, one after another, like silkworms producing never-ending silk thread. It was unsettling. Fan came home just as she was feeling irritated.

As usual he wanted to eat out. Still affected by a sense of annoyance, she did not really want to go, but she knew she'd feel empty if she stayed home. So they went out and hailed a taxi for a Zhongshan Road restaurant opened after the war by a man from Shanghai. It was filled with young Shanghainese women and modish young men, all enjoying a feast. Taking the menu proffered by a waiter, Fan asked Yulan what she'd like. Since she knew nothing about food from China, he explained dishes and ordered whatever sounded good to her. Soon their table was laden with delicacies from the mountains and the seas, plate after plate, bowl after bowl of delicious food. She was full after sampling a few dishes, while Fan kept shoveling food into his mouth, his gluttonous manner a sight to behold. Chinese food enjoys admirers all over the world, and she was no exception. They left the restaurant shortly to stroll down the street, where she saw how innocent children were affected by Japan's defeat. Sad-looking elementary school kids out selling cigarettes would pester a passerby.

"Please buy a pack, Mister."

The pleading voice, an audio illustration of their impoverished lives, was heartrending. After turning into South Gate, she saw Japanese setting up stalls on the roadside to sell their furniture and other odds and ends, all belongings and cherished items they had accumulated over decades of hard work. Now that their country had suffered defeat, none of them seemed to value what they had any longer. It was easy to imagine what they were going through, and feel sorry for them. Ah, the vile effects of war spared no one, including the innocent. Those who were pro-war perished along with those against it, all collateral damage, she said to herself.

Then she noticed the sorrowful look on the face of every Japanese around her. What was most shocking was how quickly their skin took on a distressed, sallow patina. Girls with tender skin, recently married young women, female intellectuals, and housewives were all sitting on straw mats by the road selling items from their houses, including elegant tea chests, braziers, and metal cans from the south. There were even valuable calligraphic scrolls by the Buddhist monk Kukai or paintings by Yokoyama Taikan, which were being snapped up by greedy opportunists. When they saw what was happening, the Japanese had to suppress their emotions, but sad tears and unspeakable anger were clearly visible in their eyes. The faces of their children reddened when their toys were bought and taken away, and little girls were getting dark under a blistering summer sun shining down on the treeless ground. The war had only recently ended, and yet it seemed that every Japanese suddenly looked ten years older. Yulan found it simply incredible.

The cheap wares set Fan Hanzhi on a buying spree; sometimes he bought three of the same thing. Yulan thought they didn't need to buy that many, no matter how much he liked them, but he had his reasons. He knew that inflation was inevitable, and that he must quickly convert cash into material goods. Blinded by greed, he behaved like a typical, contemptible businessman, and she found that loathsome. She saw nothing gentlemanly about her husband, who went out every day bargain-hunting, for he was only interested in material gains. How odious! It occurred to her that everyone was robbing anyone who was in serious trouble. Humans are greedy by nature, which is why there are wars. Instead of coming to a spot just to feel uneasy, it was more meaningful to sit on a bench in a park or the botanical garden and talk about life. And yet . . . as she recalled, she was reminded of one bright, moonlit night, when she could not sit still at home and asked Fan to go with her to Chuanduan. By the levee, the Xindian River flowed silently; under a bluish moonlight, the hills were hazy but still visible in the tranquil night. As a nocturnal breeze cooled her warm cheeks, she wanted to keep walking, but Fan wasn't interested. Saying it was cheerless, he wanted to turn back, so she had to leave with him. He was much more interested in such bustling areas as West Gate Market or Rongding, which he never tired of visiting. He paid close attention to shop windows and always asked about the price when he saw anything new or rare. Her husband's interest was commerce-related, completely different from her ideal kind of life. She was not only disgusted but actually pained when she saw him hunting for Japanese goods at bargain prices.

"That's enough. Let's go home. We have no more room for all this stuff."

"But it's so cheap. See this pot, how nice it is?" he said, and bought it.

Yulan was fed up with his material cravings. He'd already bought six of the same pots. One was nice, but three or four together looked terrible; that was just common sense. She was increasingly troubled by objects; for one thing, they had no more room. Irritably, she insisted they go home. He finally sensed her mood and went home with her.

They turned toward Eryuding at Zuojiujianding, where they ran into an old friend of Fan's, a fashionable middle-aged man. Fan made the introductions, telling her it was an old schoolmate. The three of them walked down the street together and, when they neared Qiansuiding, they saw a fruit stand displaying golden yellow, delicious-looking bananas. With great interest, the man picked the nicest bunch for the vendor to weigh. The vendor placed it on a scale and said it weighed two *jin*, but the man did not believe him. He kept telling the vendor to weigh it again, and the vendor did, despite his annoyance. The man still would not accept the answer and insisted on another weighing, which nettled the man, who was losing his patience as he put the bunch on the scale and explained the mechanism by pointing at the needle. Finally, Fan's friend understood, and looked at the scale curiously for a while. Yulan had no idea what he was thinking. Then he took off his hat and put it on the scale to watch the needle move, in amazement. After that, he weighed his wallet, which seemed even more fun to him. The next to be weighed were his watch and then his eyeglasses, before exclaiming loudly,

"This is great, just great. I've never seen something like this."

He asked if the man would sell the scale, a bizarre question that stunned Yulan into speechlessness. Fan had said he was a respectable gentleman, a section chief in some government office. She couldn't help but feel pessimistic about Taiwan's future; obviously a rumor that had been circulating was not entirely false. Not long ago, some schoolmates came to visit her, they'd said something similar.

"Was your husband surprised when he first saw water flow from a tap, Yulan?"

"No, why?"

"The Chinese were all flabbergasted when they saw water flowing out of the wall. Haven't you heard?"

"How could that be?"

"But the young section chief who lives near us was yelling about the wall producing water when he saw the tap."

"Aiya! That's weird. Who told you that?"

"His cook," her friend had replied with a scornful look.

"There's something even funnier, Yulan," another woman joined in. "They put their shoes in the bedroom and sleep in a storage closet. Isn't that funny?"

They chatted disdainfully, and Yulan knew what they were talking about. Their conversation turned into a critique of the Chinese, while, as if to mock her, they brought up without a qualm everything they'd heard since they were schoolmates. When taking over a certain secondary technical school, the principle was frightened by the roar of the motor when the students turned on the factory machines affiliated with the school. Backing up a good three paces, he was shaking, but managed to say, "That's good, very good, best in Asia." Everyone had a good laugh over the frightened principal. After that, the women vied to share gossip.

"This is what I've heard. A certain high school teacher said he'd studied in Germany, and proudly introduced the newest math in the world to the students, who had actually learned it in middle school. They were stunned."

"That's nothing. There's this guy in my company who said he'd studied in Japan but can't speak a word of Japanese."

"He's one of those coffee-house students."

They continued to talk and laugh. A teacher at an advanced training class, after reading off his notes in finance, smugly told the students to ask him anything they wanted. One stood up and asked about Taiwan's financial state, and the teacher had no answer. He didn't come back to teach the next day. A female teacher at a school got famous by eating and walking at the same time on campus. Someone walked onto the tatami at an elite family's house in mud-spattered shoes. Yulan's friends rattled off one story after another. At a forum with tea farmers, a technician told the growers to switch from Oolong tea to black tea, making them laugh so much they nearly fell out of their chairs. When Yulan recalled these comical anecdotes, she realized that she remembered them all and could not help getting emotional. Everything is beautified when one is in love, and the shortcomings are blotted out by the colorful rainbow of romance. Yulan was no exception. She hadn't gotten to know Fan well before they were married, for she was more interested in chasing after pretty illusions. She'd had no time to observe him; all she'd wanted was to see him every day, and she was so happy when they were together that she let her emotions get the better of her. She couldn't step back, let alone observe him calmly. Everything happened so fast and was simplified, so naturally she hadn't asked any questions. During those days she was giddily in love, but marriage is like life's alarm clock. After the wedding, she found herself with space in her mind and began to react, especially because she had nothing to do after her husband left for work. Her empty mind was taken over by all sorts of thoughts. With no one to talk to and nothing to do, the anguish from boredom became unbearable. Slowly, she began to feel the fatigue of love, for there was nothing else to pursue; the beautiful rainbow of dreams vanished after her wedding, replaced by annoying reality as it reared its ugly head. Romance is a love struggle, while marriage shackles romance. Everything would be fine if she could be content in the shackles of love, but she was nagged by dissatisfaction and the urge to break through rose now and then.

9

Several months passed in a dream-like state. During this period, the excitement over the retrocession slowly cooled; theoretically, the Taiwanese should have felt even closer to the Chinese, but reality proved the opposite. Dissatisfaction rose daily, and antagonism was widespread. Yulan, however, knew nothing about that.

One night, after they left a dance hall, a breeze cooled the stifling heat as they turned into Bending from Rongding to go home. There was no rickshaw, likely because it was too late. So, they walked home, hand in hand, down a street that looked different from daytime; the buildings seemed taller than usual, and the sounds of their footsteps, surprisingly loud, broke the silence that would be more common in a deep valley. After they rounded a street corner, they heard a sad voice selling sticky rice snacks. It was a barefoot boy of nine or ten, carrying a tin bucket, looking for buyers late into the night. Yulan felt so sorry she wanted buy all he had. When she saw there were only three left, she was trying to decide whether to buy or not, when Fan voiced his disapproval from behind,

"Why do you want to buy something like that?"

Frightened by his curt tone, the child hurried off, but soon was singing in a loud, unrestrained voice,

"Snoring after filling the belly, snoring when sleepy, hillbilly, hillbilly."

The slightly frantic doggerel bounced off the walls and sent an echo to rend the late-night tranquility, making her freeze in her path. She felt as if she'd been reproached by her own brother, but Fan didn't seem to notice anything as he walked on with a haughty air. She continued to hear the pitiful plea about the snack and see the barefoot, unsightly boy before her. She couldn't help but sense the contradiction between the boy and herself dancing the night away or her friends, who raised the roof in restaurants. The streetlights seemed lonely as they shone down, she noticed; all around them was deathly quiet so late at night.

Out of boredom she went out shopping with the maid the next day. Her new qipao might have been too long, or she simply wasn't used to wearing it, for the hem made it hard to walk, as if her legs were wrapped in the material. There was more stock in the stores, and items that had disappeared during the war were back on display. It had been a long time since she'd come to the open market. She noted that Chinese had replaced the Japanese as shoppers. She strolled around, with nothing special to buy, so she told the maid to get some greens. As they came out, some passing students chided,

"Be a concubine if you want money. Snore when sleepy, snort after filling the belly, play mahjong, have a meal, going to a show. Isn't that a great life?"

She hated talk like that, hated being mocked like that. They were young, but their tongues were sharp; they seemed both disgusted by and envious of her marriage. Marriage was the product of love, she said to herself, and love has no borders. One must make the leap, whether it's the Alps or Kunlun shan. Society, however, still suffered the effects of tradition, abhorring anything new. She was incensed when she thought about what they'd just said, "be a concubine if you want money," so she focused her thoughts on what had been happening at home. More businessmen were showing up to engage in whispered conversations with her husband, to her dismay.

Fan did not come home until very late one night; reeking of alcohol, he walked in with a red face. He was more talkative than usual as he slurred his words,

"Yulan, society is a business world and a theater. Anyone who has ideas will be rich. When people spout words like country, loyalty, or righteousness, they're just thinking about their jobs. Anyone who attacks a government official wants his job but can't get it, and people who complain about corruption are mostly their underlings. In any case, the world is filled with contradictions. Some of the idealists from the May Fourth Movement turned into corrupt officials, and even a revolutionary makes mistakes. If Confucius were alive today, he'd probably be accused of corruption, and Jesus could be taken as a war criminal. Many of Confucius' descendants are corrupt, and Jesus's followers are international arms manufacturers and murderers. Taiwan is truly a wonderful place, Yulan. Someone can come here from Chongqing with only the clothes on his back and quickly become a millionaire or a high official. Isn't that just great?"

He was spewing ideas that did not interest Yulan in the least. Her mood plunged when she recalled what he'd said about a certain degree of foolishness necessary to be loyal, filial, virtuous, and righteous. In the meantime, she was surprised by his lack of patriotism, and became keenly aware of the distance between her way of thinking and his tendency to treat everything as a business transaction; it was an unshakable contradiction. As Fan staggered into the bedroom, he dropped his briefcase and littered the floor with several carved seals. She picked them up and saw that none were his; they were all for one shop or another. That was odd, but she didn't think much about it until she was putting them back into the briefcase. It was filled with seals. Where did they all come from? She was shocked. When she asked him, he mumbled something as he lurched off. "Those? They're treasures belonging to officials. Without their seals, you can't even ride in a car."

He said this with a self-mocking smile. Yulan was confused and pressed him for details, but none were forthcoming. She had a vague sense that her husband was engaged in something illegal. He fell onto the bed and was soon snoring away. Yulan, on the other hand, was plagued with thoughts, and events from the past emerged again. The more she thought about them, the more clear-headed she was. She couldn't sleep, while Fan was snoring louder and louder as the night deepened.

She was suddenly reminded of their honeymoon trip.

It was at the Jiayi train station, where a man in a neat suit and a Shanghai flair, got on board with a suitcase. He stepped on the seat with his shoes on while putting his suitcase in the meshed, overhead compartment; the seat was soiled by his shoe prints, so he took out a tissue to wipe off the dirt before sitting down.

When they reached the Tainan station, he climbed onto the seat again to bring the suitcase down and walked off, leaving the prints behind. Those prints replayed thousands of years of history, impossible to wipe off and grating on her nerves.

Then when the conductor came to check the tickets somewhere near Changhwa, the man sitting in front of her ran to the third-class compartment but returned to second-class once the conductor left. She was left speechless over the man's shameless act. And yet he bought and ate snacks from the moment he boarded, and a quick calculation would make the cost several times more than the higher ticket price.

As these incidents occurred to her, she sensed the sorrow of the time. Her husband could not hide his true self behind the refined manner he'd copied from foreigners. To her, he had the same ugly residue on his personality, and her recollection of the days since their marriage assaulted her nerves and puzzled her. Not long ago, she had thought her husband was an exceptional man, one to be respected. How had she come to such a conclusion? No matter how she unraveled the thread of memories, an answer eluded her. It seemed obvious that he was ill-bred, vulgar, and devoid of virtues.

Back when she was a nurse, a Japanese doctor had once proposed to her. He was in love with her, and she was not put off by him. He was young, handsome, and well brought up, a medical doctor who could easily have become a college professor. But her feelings had not developed into a romantic relationship, hindered by something in her subconscious. As she thought about it now, she realized that the Japanese doctor was absolutely as good as her husband, better even, but . . . Why was she still enamored of her husband at this point in time? She didn't know. Her thoughts touched upon her emotional state just after the war. Motherland, ah, a word closer to her than even her parents. Now she saw it was that feeling that had led to her admiration for Fan. Ah, she was, after all . . .

10

The summer heat was slowly losing its intensity, and the sky grew clearer by the day. Datun shan had gained some autumn color and beauty when Yulan finally awoke from the giddiness of a newlywed.

"After experiencing it, now I can truly say men aren't so special after all. In fact, they're interesting only when you don't know them."

Boredom led her once again to miss the days before she was married. It wasn't that anything had happened to her in her current life, just that she was out of sorts and discontented. Her husband, on the other hand, cared about nothing but money, whether he was asleep or awake, afflicted with a hunger for money that went beyond need. In her view, he was simply born to make money, of which she'd been only dimly aware during the blissful state of their engagement and early days of their marriage. When she finally came out of it, she was put off by his vulgar tendency toward profiteering and his lack of a gentlemanly manner. Sometimes, she felt he was odious, distasteful. In particular, he was interested in playing mahjong, eating out, and going to movies, all lowly forms of entertainment to gratify the senses. They were a far cry from her wholesome philosophy of life. Their different views toward a variety of matters created an unbridgeable gulf. She did not know when she lost interest in going to theaters, dance halls, and restaurants, and favored staying home quietly to arrange flowers, listen to tasteful music, or take a tranquil walk. But Mr. Fan could not be enticed into sharing these activities with her. A phonograph record might be playing refined music, but he could not appreciate it, and when they were out for a walk, he found it too quiet and lacking excitement. He was just a man who preferred noisy places and festive scenes.

All this slowly exposed his true colors as a money-grubber. She remained the same, dreamy, in pursuit of lovely ideals, living in a fantasy world. So she started to bring the outside world into her life again. After neglecting the newspaper for a while, she began to pay attention to current affairs. An anti-corruption movement was in full swing, reports of which left an indescribable impression on her.

One morning Huiying paid her a surprise visit. Her friend looked pale, much different than before. She had pretty much stopped coming after marrying the Shanghai man, so they hadn't seen each other for a long time. But when they met again, they felt the same intimacy as the old days, when they were schoolmates and close friends. Huiying sobbed when she saw Yulan, forgoing small talk.

"I feel so bad, Yulan. Someone has informed against my husband."

"What do you mean?"

After a long sigh, Huiying gave her a quick account. It was quite complicated, and Yulan did not get the whole picture, only that Huiying's husband had taken some money, essentially bribery. She could not think of what to say to comfort her friend. Huiying's lips were quivering when she finished, saying she was ashamed to face the world, and threw herself into Yulan's lap to sob pitifully. Like an older sister, Yulan rubbed her friend's back and said compassionately,

"It is what it is, dear Huiying. It's fate."

Yulan continued with more comforting words while Huiying continued to weep. She stopped after a while and pointed at her belly,

"I wish I weren't carrying this, Yulan."

She sat up and cradled her belly to show Yulan that she was in her fifth or sixth month, before switching to self-mockery,

"Tell me, how can I give birth to a corrupt official's child?"

She wept again. Yulan ran out of things to say and cried with her. She felt especially glum when Huiying left. What had happened to her friend could easily happen to her one day. She could not help but worry when she thought about the kind of people Fan associated with. A couple of months earlier, two of his friends had come from Shanghai, both well-dressed, who seemed to be intellectuals but acted like common merchants. They were engaged in long discussions about something, likely ways to make money. Yulan paid them no heed back then. But now, after Huiying's visit, she had to keep her eyes open. The two men returned one night, and the three men went into another room to have a whispered conversation. They stopped when Yulan came in. She feigned ignorance and chatted for a few moments before walking out. Then she came back to eavesdrop outside.

"It was really dangerous, Chief. Japanese security was so tight we were left with no choice but to try something different. We decided to storm through the blockade but were ordered to stop. We were at a dead end until Big Nose gave the order to let us pass. Who can say why, but it was like seeing a Buddha in Hell, you know. A miracle. When we got near a port by Kaohsiung, the Coast Guard spotted us. We didn't know what to do but run for our lives. They were faster. Then we saw three rafts floating near the shore, like they'd fallen from the sky or risen out of the water. It was a godsend, so we loaded everything onto the rafts and sailed up to a poor fishing village. The autumn wind was bleak, and everywhere we looked silver grass flowers swayed in the wind. The fishermen's houses were all run-down. We took a chance and stashed the stuff there. With no good means of transportation, it took us two days to walk to a small town, where we hired a truck to find our way to K town. Luck wasn't with us, you know, because our boats, the most important things, were confiscated and we didn't have a pass, so we had to negotiate with them. They're ruthless. They want three million. We're stuck."

They continued in hushed voices. Nocturnal silence returned as they appeared to have wrapped up their report. Hearing nothing more, she sneaked back to her room just as the visitors were leaving. After mulling over what she'd heard, she concluded that it was about smuggling, but that's all she knew. After the men left, she questioned her husband, but he refused to tell her anything. She felt so alone. Not being in his confidence was more upsetting than observing his secretive behavior. How could there be secrets between husband and wife? It was against everything she believed in, which made her feel helpless and lost. She even felt that all men were liars, and that women were victimized by their lies. Resentment grew, and she felt a profound meaninglessness as a woman.

She was in an unspeakable funk the next day. After Fan left for work, she was laden with anxiety. No matter what she did, she was irritable and troubled, as if she had been forsaken by everyone. With waves of intense loneliness assailing her, she was unsettled by a stifling feeling in her chest, when Huiying came by again.

On the day after someone informed against Huiying's husband, their house was seized. Formerly Japanese property, it had been taken from them. Huiying had to go back to her parents' house; the pain was too great, so she thought she'd come visit an old friend to keep from brooding. They poured their hearts to each other and wept. To forget all their troubles, they went for a walk at Yuan shan, in order to avoid the busy downtown. Zhongshan North Road wasn't crowded, and they met no one they knew. Standing by the Zhongshan Bridge, they looked into the distance at Jiantan, where dark green water flowed lazily. A small boat bobbed in a breeze, reminding Yulan of the trip to Sun Moon Lake and the boat ride, which brought back memories of better days. When they'd had enough of the lake view, Huiying suggested they go to the zoo. Yulan went along since she had nothing better to do.

Since it was a weekday, the zoo was sparsely populated, with only a few adults and some children too young to be in school. The place had a quiet, autumnal feel. They strolled along a guided path, but neither was interested in the docile small animals. Soon they reached the elephant enclosure. The underfed animal stirred its colossal body as if to ingratiate itself with the visitors. Without thinking, Yulan went up and stared into its tiny eyes as it raised its trunk to pick up crackers that children had tossed it. It chewed slowly, a sight that elicited gleeful shouts from its feeders. Similarly, delighted adults also flung fruit in, encouraging the elephant to step up its fawning show to curry favor. It was just like humans. Yulan was taken aback by that realization. An elephant acted like a sycophant for food, playing up to the crowd. Aiya! Are we women like elephants? Enclosed in a cage called "family," an object for her husband to look at. Disgust rose inside her at the thought. The elephant continued to swing its trunk and squint to butter up the visitors. An intense sense of loathing made her hurry off and head to a hill, where they sat on a bench. Huiyi was probably tired, as she sat there silently, while Yulan fixed her gaze on the distant scenery.

The view was fantastic. The Keelung River flowed slowly around green fields with verdant rice shoots like emerald waves, before which stood the graceful Guanyin shan, its low ridge sloping to both sides. It was a mirage of the early days of her marriage: if her husband were promoted to a high position, she would, in a few years' time, get to enjoy the flowers on Zijin shan with the wives of important government officials. Now that was destined to be only a dream. She lingered to admire a view she never tired of seeing. Then it occurred to her that her husband might be in the same position as Huiying's. What would she do if that happened? She could not stop worrying, when her gaze fell on Huiying's protruding belly. A strange thought flashed through her mind: Was that the baby of a corrupt official? She froze when she recalled what her friend had said. But her husband was a hero who had taken part in the Northern Expedition. That was true, but . . . Ah! Something similar was squirming inside her too. What would it be? Or was it . . . Her hair stood on end. She was beset by anxiety, which in turn made her restless. The lush green scenery lost its luster. In a fit of fear and agitation, she ran down the hill, oblivious to her friend's presence.

11

Fan Hanzhi showed his true colors once the romance faded. The takeover had been chaotic, and loopholes were everywhere, all supplying opportunities for him to make money. If missed, these opportunities would never rise again, a realization that made him restless. He wanted to make a killing and leave for Hong Kong, a safe city with culture and plenty of places for fun. He did not have to stay on the small Taiwanese island. No, he could enjoy a leisurely life in an international city and show Yulan around. He wanted and needed to act quickly. Smuggling sugar was profitable, but it was hard to move a large quantity of the cargo; besides, it had become a focus of attention now, which meant he couldn't make too much from it. He wondered if there was something that he could do without anybody knowing about it and still bring in a huge amount. Taking over Japanese assets would do fine, but without knowing someone inside, it would be tough. He had to find something relatively easy. In any case, the easiest and most effective solution was to use the dozens of carved seals in his briefcase, but, unfortunately, budget caps got in the way. No matter what, he had to dream big to make it big. If you hoped for a hundred, you'd get fifty dollars, a thousand would reap five hundred, and five thousand for ten thousand. A man of worth must at least think of billions. What could he do though? Sugar, salt, tea, fruit? None of those would be good enough. He'd thought Taiwan was a treasure island, but after playing around for a while, he realized that it was a surprisingly barren place with little money to be made. Coming all this way had been a waste of time and energy. In any case, great ambition often ends with great disappointment. But Taiwan must have its worth; there had to be something unknown to everyone else. He racked his brain. As Sun Tzu wrote in *The Art of War*, knowing yourself and your enemy means total victory. In a word, he did not know Taiwan; that is, he did not know enough people to make things easy. So, he had to work with the locals; otherwise, he'd be left empty-handed, even if he was allowed into the treasure trove. Right, he said to himself, he had to use the locals.

A happy smile broke out on his face when he reached that conclusion. He was amused by his failure to come up with a solution until now. Making connections with the locals would surely be faster than working on any other channels. He had been socializing with locals but had never thought of putting those contacts to use, a grave mistake on his part. Right, there was Big Nose Qian, who had been coming for permits lately. He should work with Qian and give the man a chance to make some money.

Time to act.

One day Qian walked in with a grin.

"What's on your mind, Qian?"

"There's something . . ."

The man seemed hesitant.

"Is there someplace we can talk, Chief?" he whispered.

A fawning smile was a sign that he needed help.

"Here's my chance," Fan said to himself and immediately agreed to go out.

They went to a restaurant in Xinqiding and started drinking. After they'd had a few, Qian broached the subject,

"During the Japanese occupation, I was an imperial merchant, but had trouble making money until rationing began after war broke out. I got to know a Japanese officer who took care of everything. Needless to say, I was able to get my hands on rationed goods and had a special channel for things not readily available. Buying and selling supplies for the military was a terrific trade in those days. In the year before the war ended alone, I made a killing, so I supplied the Japanese officer with everything he needed when he was sent back home, and that made him very happy. Now the war is over, and my connection has been lost. I'm still trying to find a new one. I went to see a few section chiefs but came away with nothing. Zhongshan Road isn't easy to travel, too many roadblocks. For example, the chief of Section A might say yes, but the chief of Section B would say no. I'd work very hard on B to get his permission, but then something else would crop up to block my way. It's tough doing business in a situation like this." He finished with a sigh.

"That's a misconception on your part, Qian," Fan said with a smile. "There may be many side streets spoking off Zhongshan Road, but there's only one Zhongshan Road. If you keep going, you'll get to where you want to be. You just don't know the key words. Fan fixed his eyes on the mans' face. "The key is this."

He drew a circle with his fingers. Qian surely knew that money was vital but did not know how to use it. Fan lowered his voice and whispered the important words to Qian. Following his advice, though with trepidation, Qian tried out Fan's idea the next day. Taking an audacious friend along to Section A, he followed Fan's suggestion by presenting a detailed price list. The chief just listened silently, sitting with a haughty air and not saying a word. Seeing that the moment had arrived, Qian's friend quietly offered the man a small notebook. The chief continued to sit primly as he glanced at the notebook. He nodded.

"Okay."

He stamped the application with a seal.

"A hundred thousand as compensation for the chief," was written on the notebook.

Finally, Qian realized that this was the way to walk down Zhongshan Road. Following his success, he went to see the chiefs of Sections B and C, as well as the head of accounts receivable. Smooth sailing, with no roadblocks. Finally, he fully grasped what Fan had meant by only one Zhongshan Road, despite all the side streets. It had seemed complicated but turned out to be astonishingly easy. He was thrilled for the first time in recent memory. His worries gone, he decided to drink the night away at a café.

Fan was right about Qian, who acted quickly and moved nimbly. Whatever he worked on, Qian could produce results right away.

Suddenly reminded of Taiwan's forests, Fan told Qian to look into it. He was surprised to read about the quantity and variety: vast numbers of Japanese cypress, Taiwanese cypress, fir, plum, camphor, cedar, and others. It was like an inexhaustible treasure, a great deal of virgin forest untouched by an axe. The government had a set price that was lower than market value, which meant a profit of two hundred for every six kilos, two million dollars for ten thousand kilos, and two hundred million for a hundred thousand kilos. It was an incredibly profitable business. A while back, Qian had told him about ten thousand kilos of lumber stashed near a water source. It wasn't a lot of wood, and there was a potential problem, so nothing was done about it. In the end, someone moved faster and found a way to sell it. Fan then told Qian to check out the trees on Taiping and Baxian mountains, and expected to hear from him soon. Speed was the key in everything these days unless one wanted to lose out. Qian had a mentality problem about the conservation forest, saying the trees there should be kept, or the people would suffer if there were a flood. They needed to act quickly on this, in Fan's view, but Qian was constantly under the threat of such a strange concept. Obviously, he did not understand that there is no morality where money is concerned. Fan was sure everyone would come to that realization soon; these people hadn't experienced the turbulence in China, so were often timid even in trivial matters. The Taiwanese were smart but had no guts; they looked clever but were still Taiwanese, after all, with little ambition. Fan wished he could find a way to change him.

Qian returned a few days later, and they met for a drink at the usual place.

"I've got good news, Chief. The Japanese had a forest protection policy that divided the mountain areas into districts, with strict laws against unauthorized cutting. Even when it was allowed, we could only cut a certain percentage of the trees. Which is why there are pots of gold all over the forest. Verdant old growth hidden in the clouds and mist is a secret in Taiwan, and all we need is a little of it."

Qian was shouting when he finished. He raised his glass and toasted Fan, who clinked his glass with a meaningful smile. They were in high spirits. Fan exploded into a drunken outburst,

"I'm surprised you have such simple desires, Old Qian. You should dream big. There are plenty of opportunities to make money, and it's not too late to start today. Take the factories that were handed over to us, for example. They can't all be run by the central or provincial governments. They'll soon be auctioned off. When that happens, you buy, even if the price is high. If you don't have the money to run the factories, you use them as collateral for a bank loan for something else. We're suffering from inflation now, so whatever you borrow can be used to buy commodities. In two or three months, the commodity price will double, and the million you borrowed will net a million, while a hundred million will bring another hundred million. You'll still be making money, even if your factory stops running. Which is why some cunning fellows have stopped work at the factories they seized and use them to make a bundle. What do you say, Qian?"

Fan stopped to give him a sinister smile before continuing,

"With a factory, you'll also have additional revenue. This is how it is, Qian. There are many companies run by the central and provincial governments. If you can get your hands on whatever they have and sell it on the black market, you'll strike it rich. For example, you apply to purchase cement or other materials in the name of factory maintenance or expansion. Most of what you see on the market came about this way."

Fan was talking up a storm, enlightening Qian on things he'd never heard before. Qian echoed Fan's ideas loudly,

"Right. You're so right. Actually, some Taiwanese have been saying that we'll know where corruption is occurring simply by rationing a particular item."

He went on to share what he'd heard.

"Let's not talk about that, but I think we ought to bid on a factory."

Qian groaned silently when Fan cavalierly ignored the topic of corruption; he was somewhat fearful, in fact. They returned to the subject of buying lumber and worked out the details before leaving.

Qian began buying up lumber. Having learned how to travel down Zhongshan Road, he settled on one particular forest district.

He had no trouble getting a permit, by offering fifteen dollars per six kilos as compensation, but he had trouble obtaining cutting rights, no matter what he did. He was left with no choice but to get back in touch with Fan. After dispensing some money, he swaggered into the forestry district with a permit and cutting rights. But then the onsite director drank all day and ignored him. So he had to go back and find the necessary connections, with the help of money, of course.

One day Qian invited the onsite director to go drinking, along with a few Taiwanese. Since they were in the mountains, he could only find a few village girls as drinking companions. They were local, but their beauty was unsurpassed, fairy ladies, in fact, to men who had lived away from women in the mountains. They drank and talked and laughed with the girls, talking and singing, singing and talking. Great fun was had by all until dawn, when the Ddirector said drunkenly,

"You're a smart man, Qian." He reached over to shake Qian's hand in a firm grip.

"Take this with you. It's too much trouble for me to follow you in the mountains, so you do it yourself. Remember not to cut any trees that are under fifteen years old."

He had handed Qian the approval stamp for checking tree ages; the rule stipulated that any tree fifteen years or younger must not be cut. Qian thanked him with more toasts. The director was in a great mood and, clinking his glass with Qian, said in a low voice,

"It really doesn't matter how much . . ."

He then gave Qian some pointers before they went their separate ways jovially.

Qian went into the mountains the next day with lumbermen. Old-growth trees stood like masts on ships; the forest was dark, even during daytime. Those under fifteen years old could fetch a pretty price too, so Qian wavered. He'd spent so much time, energy, and money to get where he was now, why should he hold back? he said to himself. He told the lumbermen to stamp those under fifteen if they looked good enough. The stamped ones would then be cut down. After he worked out the process in his head, he gave them the go ahead while he sat on a high ground to watch. Sounds of stamping rose and swirled in the mountain, returning to silence once the echoes vanished. There were towering trees as far as the eye could see, all seemingly dispassionately relating their stories over centuries. Spurred by the mystery of the trees, he was reminded of the possibility of severe flooding if the trees were all cut down. Feeling bad, he considered saving the smaller ones when he heard the sounds of stamping all around. He suffered a momentary attack of a guilty conscience, but on the other hand, he had come so far, and if he didn't go all the way, he might not have a second chance to finish it off. What Fan had said came to his rescue, "There is no morality where money is concerned."

He repeated it several times.

Fan's plan was being carried out step by step. But just when success was at hand, he was, after all, not a god, and his evil deeds came to light.

As a secret service section chief, he'd gotten to know a Japanese army officer. Being a military man, the officer knew nothing except his drink. Fan sent two of his underlings with the officer to extort wealthy merchants or well-to-do families by accusing them of spying for Chongqing. One of their targets was a rich man in Wuhu, a stubborn old man who refused to offer them money no matter how they tortured him. It created a big stir, and the officer could no longer contain it; they were left with falsifying evidence and turned him over to the Japanese secret service. The old man was a prominent, highly regarded figure in the area, so the locals worked hard to get him released. The Japanese secret service took spy cases very seriously, so Fan and his cronies held onto the false accusation. In the end, the old man was sentenced to death. After the war ended, the case was exposed, and the old man's son filed a suit against Fan. Fan's underlings were taken into custody, but Fan, the ringleader, was nowhere to be found. The government did its best to search for him, but to no avail. But they never gave up and vowed to find and arrest him.

12

When the takeover came to an end, a rumor began to circulate that many traitors from China had sneaked into Taiwan; no one knew where it came from, but it was enough to put the government on alert. Now and then a minor traitor would be grabbed, a sensational headline for newspapers. Fan grew apprehensive every time he read a piece like that. One day a friend from Shanghai came to pay him a special visit and told him about the government's active search. No matter what, he must be careful, for the government was conducting a secret but thorough investigation, his friend said. Fan thought hiding would be his best strategy for now, so, without telling his wife, he went on a trip to the south.

The government was rattled over its failure to find Fan, despite the extensive net it deployed, for his whereabouts were hard to pinpoint. The resolute leader of the search team took over as the frontline commander. In addition to train stations, he also made sure that piers and ports were closely watched to prevent Fan from slipping through. If he were to flee to Hong Kong or China, all their hard work would be in vain. The leader was a man in his fifties with high ideals; he had been active in the May Fourth Movement, had rendered great service during the Northern Expedition, and had fought all over China during the eight-year war with Japan. With such an illustrious career, he would not be discouraged by a minor setback, which, in fact, made him even more determined to succeed. This was why he had taken over the search and stationed himself at the Taipei Train Station. He checked intelligence reports sent from all parts of the island while watching the station carefully. Nothing fruitful came after two weeks of heightened alert. He was a patient man, but his resolve wavered and his fraut nerves were constantly on the verge of snapping.

It was the fifteenth day of his watch. Passengers swarmed onto the platform when the northbound train pulled in. Redcaps were busy moving cargo here and there. The leader saw a well-dressed young man detrain from a third-class car and quickly disappear into the crowd. The suspicious behavior caught his attention and, as a reflex, he followed the young man. Once reaching the top of the stairs, the man turned and shoved his way to the other side. The exit was jam-packed, so the leader had time to race up like a bird and check against the picture he carried. When he was sure it was indeed Fan Hanzhi, whom he'd spent a whole hard year searching for, he ordered Fan to stop and easily took him into custody. As if giving up hope, Fan did not put up a fight, but meekly surrendered. A commotion broke out around them. What's happening? People were wondering. Something felt different, but the crowd quieted down quickly. It was quieter than Fan could have imagined, and that scared him. As he was led down the stairs in front of the station, vendors selling ice pops, noodles, sticky rice snacks, and cigarettes all came up to gawk. Someone yelled out,

"Watch out! Cops!" followed by more shouts, "Grab the cigarettes!" "Hurry, run."

The shouts sounded sad and helpless, while cigarette vendors ran off in all directions like skittering spiders. Then a truck roared up and came to sudden stop; two uniformed men jumped off and grabbed the cigarettes and money from those who did not get away fast enough. Fan turned to smile slyly at the leader and muttered, as if to himself, "If you sell out the country for personal gains you're called a traitor, but what do you call a government official who cheats the people to benefit himself?" He gave the leader a meaningfully ironic and sinister smile.

The search team erupted in happy cheers when they returned to headquarters; the leader was the only one who looked unsettled and unhappy. Having decided to write a report, he checked Fan's background. The more he read, the more astonished he was. Fan had earned merits during the Northern Expedition and had performed splendidly as a secret agent in the early days of war with Japan, quite similar to Chen Deqing (Huiying's husband), who had been informed on days earlier. They both had glorious pasts. Flabbergasted by the extreme contradictions, he grew fatigued and closed his aging eyes as he let his thoughts continue. He was about to doze off, as the faces of old friends who had been part of the May Fourth Movement flashed before his eyes. Time had passed so quickly. It had been more than three decades. The resourceful ones were now heading government ministries. How many of his old friends were in high positions now? Chen, Huang, Xu, Liu . . . Then there were some who had taken the wrong path. He was shocked when he counted them. Ten were traitors; eighteen were corrupt officials. His eyes snapped open from disbelief. His secretary walked in with a grin and congratulated the leader for nabbing Fan. The grinning face looked just like Fan's. Then he saw that everyone in the office, even the janitor, was grinning like that, their faces the spitting images of the traitors and corrupt officials who had been informed on. It was loathsome. For a moment he had the illusion that a great many of the country's population were traitors and corrupt officials.

2

JIAN A-TAO

A SON OF TAIWAN

Ye Shitao
(translated by Craig A. Smith)

For the Sad Story of Luku

Jian A-tao had finished his piping hot bowl of sweet congee shortly after ten in the morning when a soldier appeared at his cell door and shouted: "Inmate 3002, Let's go!" All prisoners were given numbers in the Counterintelligence Bureau secret prison in the former Takasago Steel Mill. 3002 was Jian A-tao's.

Gazing at that big, tasty pot of sweet congee, cooked with sugar and nonfat milk powder from American AID packages, A-tao was reluctant to step away from it.

He stood up and walked unhappily to the door. "Stop!" the soldier shouted. "Bring all your things!"

An ominous feeling rose from the pit of his stomach. A-tao raised his voice as he answered back: "You only said 'present yourself.' How was I supposed to know I was to bring my things?"

"Watch your mouth and get a move on!" the soldier shouted impatiently and then ignored him.

"Where are you taking him, friend?" an old mainland Chinese prisoner, who was friendly with Jian A-tao, asked the soldier amiably.

"He'll be fine. We're just moving him to the back row," the soldier replied, not dropping his cool indifference.

So it was just a cell transfer, probably nothing to get worked up about. The knot that had formed in A-tao's stomach loosened as his mood brightened. He quickly bundled his bedding, clothes, and few belongings into an old army blanket, though he was still reluctant to leave the cell where he'd spent nearly six months. He and his cellmates were like brothers, and they had taken good care of him. He had no desire to leave this cell for something unfamiliar. It would take a long time to gain this level of camaraderie with other prisoners. And he was in the front row, which received longer hours of sunshine and was less humid, so inmates here had fewer skin diseases. Worst of all, he'd be deprived of his only comfort: This cell was just within reach of the women's prison, and every morning he could watch the female prisoners walk past his cell to wash their faces and brush their teeth. The consolation and happiness he felt in those moments was like an elixir sustaining his continued existence. Each was like a blossoming rose, reminding him that there are still some things of beauty worth lingering in this world for.

Jian A-tao roused himself to bid farewell to each of his cellmates. He was aware that this farewell would be their last. There would never be an opportunity to meet again. If he was not dead in a year, most of his friends left in this cell would be. Their next meeting could only be in the afterlife.

Lowering his head and following the soldier, he turned a corner and walked for three or four minutes before arriving at the third row of cells. Even during the day, it was so dark you couldn't see your hand in front of your face. Each cell was lit by a bare ten-watt bulb that burned like an altar lamp in hell. Wordlessly, the solider opened the door and shoved

Jian A-tao

A-tao inside, not leaving him any chance to talk back. Unaccustomed to the lack of light, he stumbled and nearly fell. He sat on the floor to let his eyes grow accustomed to the darkness.

The cell was more spacious than the previous one, perhaps 350 square feet. They could probably squeeze more than thirty prisoners into such a cell, but in the dim light he could make out only five or six. What was going on? Was this some form of kindness, letting him have room to sleep, more space for him to move about, maybe do some physical exercise? The thought made him laugh to himself.

Just at that moment he noticed Professor Wang Jiesheng among the people in the room. Wang recognized him at the same time and walked over excitedly.

"How have you been Mr. Jian!" Wang clasped A-tao's hands, happy to the point of tears.

"It's you, Professor Wang! I thought your case was closed and you'd been handed over to the military court long ago!" A-tao was noticeably surprised.

"No! They just took me to another secret prison for interrogation. I have no idea why, but today they brought me back here." The white-haired but robust old man in his sixties, the kindly former president of the Taiwan Chung Hsing Publishing house, and professor of Zhejiang University before that, spoke softly.

As they'd enjoyed chatting about 1930s Chinese literature when they'd been locked up together, they'd gotten along well, caring and watching out for each other. Wang had a serious heart condition, and A-tao had had his family send him some Kyushin tablets. When they spoke, they used Japanese to prevent any informers who might be in their cell from listening in. Wang had studied in Japan and had been friends with Lu Xun and Xu Shoushang. Of course, this was one of the principle reasons he'd aroused suspicion and was arrested.

However, the reason given for his arrest was "embezzlement." Taiwan Chung Hsing Press had been ordered to reorganize. Actually, the press was the Taiwan branch of the internationally renowned Shanghai Chung Hsing Publishing House. Wang Jiesheng had secretly sent all profits from the Taiwan office to Hong Kong, and then planned to transfer the funds back to the Shanghai main office. He refused to comprehend how important it was for the so-called "Taiwan" Chung Hsing Press to preserve its independence and persisted in his loyal adherence to orders from the Shanghai head office. This indicated a disrespect for the authorities on Taiwan.

"How's your wife? And your girl?" A-tao recalled that Wang's wife taught at the Taipei First Girls High School and that his daughter was a student at Taiwan University.

"They took back my campus housing. My wife and daughter were almost thrown out onto the street, but they're staying with friends for now. It looks like my wife won't be able to keep her teaching job. I just can't see how they'll get by in the future."

Wang Jiesheng spoke with a despondent look. A-tao worried that this searing distress could precipitate a heart attack.

"There's a Taiwanese saying that every blade of grass has its own dew. We may be helpless in prison, but we have to stay healthy and live to walk out of here if we want to bring the women any consolation." A-tao struggled to cheer him up.

The group in the prison cell had evidently been thrown together from various places on the spur of the moment. Aside from Jian A-tao and Wang Jiesheng, there was middle-aged Xu Zhongxiong, who had a bright red scar across his neck. He had been Party Secretary of the Taiwan Democratic Self-Government League's branch on Daqiu Island. After his arrest, he had tried to kill himself by slashing his jugular with a hidden razor blade. Fortunately, his life was saved. Xu's story had reached every cell, giving him a kind of legendary status. A-tao recognized him by his scar. Xu discreetly warned him about three others in the cell. A young man in his twenties with slicked-back hair was from the Hong Kong office of the Counterintelligence Bureau. Some sort of mishap resulted in his arrest and he'd been brought here. He did not at all look like a government thug. With a pious expression, he continuously read his copy of the New Testament by the dusky lamplight. Then there was a middle-aged man in a Western suit jacket who was always smiling. According to Xu, he'd been Defense Minister for the Republic of Taiwan. And finally, there was a short, stocky man who was reported to be a notorious gangster from Sanchong. He'd once owned a handgun and killed secret agents with it.

That evening Xu Zhongxiong proposed making Professor Wang a kind of cell captain to negotiate with the guards whenever necessary. Wang refused the position, arguing that he was too frail to shoulder the responsibility. Ultimately, it fell to A-tao, the logical choice, given the circumstances. Although he'd been arrested because of his involvement with the Taiwan Work Committee, he hadn't joined the Communist Party. Out of the six, each of whom was related to a different faction, he was the only one detached from and impartial to the politics of the factions. He had to accept.

As they had ample space, the six of them were free to choose places near the door. At the front of the cell, each occupied a spot close to the corridor, where they could lay out their bedding and get a good night's sleep. Now the cell captain, A-tao had to delegate tasks to ensure that the daily life of the prisoners was comfortable. He had imagined that no one would be willing to take out the chamber pot, but aside from him and Wang, the other four inmates clamored for the work. This was no surprise. Although dumping the chamber pot was a lowly and smelly task, the opportunity allowed them to go outside for a walk and fresh air, maybe pick up a cigarette butt to take back and share. They were happy to compete for this privilege.

A-tao chatted with Professor Wang for a while, but he was overstimulated by all the changes that day and was feeling drowsy, He rested his head on some books he'd stacked for a pillow just before fatigue overwhelmed him and he fell asleep.

He did not know how long he'd slept when noisy footsteps and shrill cries woke him. He sluggishly left his dream for the real world.

The bare bulb was still projecting its pale light. He rubbed his eyes and sat up on his army blanket like a helpless child before opening his eyes wide in shock at the sight in the corridor outside his cell.

A dozen or more armed soldiers escorted a group of more than thirty new prisoners, including the old and weak, men and women. At each cell, the commanding officer read off names from a register for a routine identification before cramming the prisoners into the cells. Occasionally, a confused inmate would hesitate and be roughly shoved in by a soldier's rifle butt. Some among the new prisoners were blubbering, clearly not the sort who would commit political crimes! A-tao was astonished.

"They'll arrest anyone! This time they even pulled in a bunch of destitute farmers! Bastards!" Professor Wang snorted disdainfully.

A-tao took a sober look at the scene. Wang was right. They were a ragtag bunch of barefoot, destitute farmers. Some were still wearing tattered conical farming hats. A-tao was used to seeing intellectuals brought in as political prisoners, but this was beyond imagining. Is there any way the Taiwan Communist Party's influence could have penetrated the mass of farm laborers?

After the soldiers prodded two or three prisoners into each of the cells along the way, they arrived at his cell and stopped outside with more than ten prisoners still remaining.

"Who's the cell captain?" barked the commanding officer.

"That would be me, inmate 3002!" A-tao scrambled forward.

"Find some space and get these sixteen new inmates settled. And do it right!"

The commanding officer shouted his order with authority.

"Of course! They're all our people. We'll take good care of them!" A-tao replied with more than a little sarcasm.

"Watch your mouth!" The commanding officer spat violently as he opened the cell door and kicked the fresh inmates into the cell, one by one. After the soldiers marched off, A-tao busied himself with distributing army blankets, making sure they'd be warm enough through the long cold night, although no one was likely to feel the cold with twenty-two adults sleeping in a small space. By custom, the existing inmates had the reasonable privilege of occupying the better spots at the front of the cell. However, A-tao reserved the spot beside him for a man in his seventies, even lending him his own quilt.

This new group of prisoners were an unschooled lot. One look and A-tao knew they were destitute farmers from deep in the mountains. They did not even have towels or toothbrushes, and A-tao guessed they might not be in the habit of brushing their teeth. The next morning, he realized this was not the case. They had been arrested at night in bed. They hadn't had a chance to take anything before being shoved into an armored truck and driven here.

At ten o'clock on that second day, everyone watched the new group of prisoners wolf down their breakfast. In less than fifteen minutes, each big bowl of powdered milk and sweet congee was licked clean. A few of the old inmates were stupefied by the scene.

Professor Wang, who had forgotten to eat his own meal, gladly handed it to them. "How was it?" he asked with a little laugh.

"Delicious! I've never had anything this good!" The farmers spoke almost as one.

"Humph! Too dumb to know better! Country bumpkin trash!" The gangster from Sanchong couldn't stand the sight of them: "Nobody outside this prison would touch this moldy US AID milk powder! It's only fit for pigs, but those bastards feed it to us!"

"Hey, enough already. Leave them alone. Can't you see they're so poor they've never had milk powder before?!" A-tao stopped the Sanchong gangster from going on a rant.

After their meal, they lay down to rest, since their sleep had been cut short the night before. Once he'd pulled the old army blanket over himself and the old man, curiosity got the better of him.

"What's your name, old uncle?"

"I'm Wu Jinshui, seventy-two years old," The old man spoke through belches from eating too much congee. He was skin and bones.

"Uncle Jinshui, then. Where are you from?"

"We're from Luku!" the old uncle spoke assuredly, as though everyone should know his hometown.

"Luku? And that's close to . . ."

"You don't know?" Suddenly deflated, the old man explained: "It's a mountain area south of Hsichi."

"Oh! I know it." A-tao had heard that after the disbanding of the Taiwan Work Committee, some cadres had actively established a number of guerrilla bases in the northern mountain areas under the umbrella of the Taipei Committee. Luku must have been one of those bases.

"So what were you arrested for?"

"How would I know? I didn't do anything!" Wu Jinshui spoke indignantly: "Just before dawn everyone in the village opened their doors to find armored vehicles on the hills around the village. We were surrounded. Then a bunch of soldiers with rifles jumped out and went from house to house, arresting everyone they found, no matter who they were. There are probably more than a hundred of us." The terror had not left Wu Jinshui.

"That's not what I mean. I mean did you get involved in the rebellion?"

"What's a rebellion? I don't understand. Mr. Chen from the Farmers' Association asked us to put our seal on a register for the distribution of fertilizer. Maybe that was the problem. Everyone who put their seal to it was rounded up."

A trace of cunning flitted across the face of the guileless old farmer. A-tao knew that the workers trained by the Taiwan Communist Party were adept at disguising themselves. Actually, they all held firm beliefs and unshakable resolve because they were so impoverished they weren't afraid of dying.

"Uncle Jinshui, the register that was supposed to be about the distribution of fertilizer must have been a document stating that you were joining the rebellion and the party." Jian A-tao spoke with bitterness. That alone was in violation of Article 5. If found guilty, one would serve a minimum of ten years imprisonment, but A-tao could not bring himself to say this out loud.

"Did your village have many gatherings?"

"Oh, yes. In the morning, all the villagers would attend the flag-raising ceremony in the school yard to sing the national anthem."

"The national anthem? Can you sing it for me now?"

"I'm not much of a singer. It'll be embarrassing!"

Wu Jinshui began singing in a low voice but serious tone. Although he was indeed out of tune, the melody and the rhythm were mostly correct. Hearing him sing the "national anthem," A-tao was flabbergasted, speechless, for the so-called "anthem" of the People's Republic was in fact Nie Er's "March of the Volunteers." So what flag did they raise?

"The national flag, was it a white sun in a blue sky over a field of red?"

"Not at all! It has an image of a sickle on it!"

"A sickle?" A-tao had never seen such a flag and could not imagine what it looked like. He vaguely recalled that the Soviet flag had a sickle.

"Was there someone to teach you to read and sing?"

"Yeah! He was a tall, handsome middle-aged man named Lü. He had a beautiful booming voice!"

"Your teacher's surname was Lü?" A-tao suddenly thought of the author Lü Heruo from the older generation, who had been missing for years with no news. Lü Heruo had studied music in Japan and was known for his baritone voice.

"Yeah. He had so much passion when he taught us the national anthem, plus a few other good songs. And at night he ran a class to teach us old-timers how to read."

"Then, was he arrested alongside the rest of you?"

"No. He died a long time ago."

"Died?" A-tao almost cried out in shock.

"Was it an illness?"

"No, snakebite!" A sigh escaped Wu Jinshui's lips. He quietly sobbed: "He worked so hard! He was a good man full of kindness!"

A-tao could imagine the situation after the organization was broken up. Lü Heruo likely had nowhere to hide and fled to Luku to avoid pursuit.

A-tao was so saddened by the news that he lay trembling before gradually sinking into resignation. Perhaps death was all Lü could have hoped for. Now he is buried on a hill of lush green grass, under blue skies and white clouds. Each day he passes with the sun, the breeze, the singing birds, and the smell of flowers, no longer needing to worry about the freedom and happiness of the Taiwanese people. A-tao silently said a prayer for Lü Heruo in the afterlife and promised that one day in the future he would write fiction even better than Lü's, building on his bloody sacrifice.

He didn't know how long he'd slept when he abruptly woke up. The smell of dinner told him it was already four in the afternoon. He politely poured out a big bowl of pumpkin soup for each of the new inmates, telling them to eat their fill. A happy clamor rose up as the new inmates shoved food into their mouths, smacking their lips

Days of Eating Pork Skin

I've long known about Cavalry Barracks Street in old Tainan. It's where the Yatang family home once stood. It was long gone by the time the Japanese took over Taiwan, and the local courthouse was built on the site, a building with the grand air of a colonial government office. There is no chance that my family would be in any way involved in the lawsuits filed in such a local court. We had never been involved in any lawsuits whatsoever, so, apart from occasions in which I was just passing by, it was rare for me to wander into this neighborhood. However, as fate would have it, there was a time when I practically lived on Cavalry Barracks Street.

Once night falls, Cavalry Barracks Street is covered in an impenetrable darkness, but a short way off one finds the bright lights and bustling action of the night market in front of the Lianghuang Temple. The market lies at the tail end of Ximending, close to the red-light district of Xinding, so it's full of all kinds of food stalls doing a thriving and lively business.

Every evening I'd drag my tired feet from Cavalry Barracks Street down to the temple, a full or crescent moon hanging in the western sky as I walked. As it would be close to midnight, most of the stalls would already be closed, but I never worried. I always knew that Uncle Ge Gen's stall would still be open. The things he sold were a bit different. In the big steel wok, he would slow cook things like pig skin, daikon, and fried tofu. It was kind of like a Japanese hotpot, but with different ingredients. The Japanese type included expensive ingredients, like konnyaku, tofu, taro, and kamaboko fish cakes, while Uncle Ge Gen would round up humble items that some might look down on. A big bowl cost only two *yuan*, and broth refills were free. If I had five *yuan* in my pocket, I could buy a cup of Red Label rice wine or Taibai wine, as well as a big bowl of pig skin soup to help it down. I could always wind up tipsy. But restraint is no easy matter, so more often than not I would not go home until I was dead drunk. There was a carbide lamp above the stall, so after my second cup, I would be so bleary-eyed I couldn't see Uncle Ge Gen's face. He was once an artist working in the red-light district of Xinding. They say he played an erhu to accompany Peking Opera singers, who sold their art but not their bodies. He came here to run a food stall when he was older, which is actually related to the rise and fall of Xinding. When that period of refined culture came to an end, people no longer visited Xinding to hear the geishas sing Peking opera. And the erhu players followed them into unemployment. Therefore, this old man kept the old ways, never troubling customers who owed money. But there were problems too. He never cautioned anyone not to drink too much, nor was he someone we would call generous. If you had nibbled away all the pork skin in your bowl, he'd never give you more, only adding broth. So, unless you announced you'd hand over another two *yuan*, you'd not be getting another bite of the undercooked pork rind. I never left owing him money, but some nights I couldn't cough up the extra two *yuan*. When this happened, I had to make do with just broth and wine.

This was in the 1950s. At that time, I was all alone in this world working as a temporary janitor for the Water Board, close to Cavalry Barracks Street. My daily work involved all sorts of small tasks, including running the boiler for disinfecting the testing instruments, sweeping the floors, throwing out the garbage, making tea, wiping desks, and taking things to the post office.

I worked the evening shift and wouldn't get off until about midnight. With no other way to release the bitter sadness that overwhelmed me, I could only drown my sorrows in drink.

When you're down and out, inevitably you'll let others walk all over you. In the forsaken 1950s, to be fortunate enough to come back from that damned island alive was tantamount to being blessed with God's mercy. What more could I ask for? The real problem was that like all insignificant intellectuals anywhere in the world, I had no skills to speak of. I was useless. It was only natural that I should become a janitor. It was the only way I could continue eating three meals a day. Do not imagine that I relished a Tolstoyan existence, finding honor in exchanging my labor for a loaf of bread.

I'd never heard mention of Uncle Ge Gen having a wife and children, but one night, as always, while I was sitting on a wooden stool shining with accumulated grease, I looked up and saw a young woman attentively washing dishes under a pale sliver of moon over the horizon. I was in a good mood that night, as I had just made a tidy sum on the nightshift and was ready to drink my fill, but only a buffoon would drink himself into a stupor in the presence of a young woman.

When she looked up, surprise spread across her face. She fixed me with an astonished stare but quickly turned away, leaned close to the old man, as though she was about to nibble his earlobe, and whispered something to him. He listened and said "Yeah! Yeah!" with a tone of surprise. The scene was dimly lit by the swaying carbide lamp.

"Want a drink?" he asked.

"You need to ask?" I responded testily.

Uncle Ge Gen was not offended. He picked up a big teacup and filled it with rice wine. The big cups cost four *yuan*, and I only wanted a small cup, but I didn't call him out for it. Anyway, I had enough to pay for the big cup that day. The big bowl of pork skin soup was also different from my usual bowl. It had more pork skin and less daikon than usual, and he put in more coriander and sesame oil as well, making the soup more aromatic. I buried my head in my soup and wine, forgetting about the old man and young woman. Ambition suffers under poverty, so my manners may have been unsightly. But strangely, when I'd finished the bowl of pork skin soup, the young woman filled it up again. This wasn't just broth, but pork skin and tofu as well. Then, once I'd finished my wine, she poured me another without waiting for my order. Uncle Ge Gen was busy with other customers, leaving the woman to wait only on me. Although he didn't say a word, he smiled as if to indicate that he approved of her actions. I observed it all, and dark thoughts suddenly took shape in my mind: I thought the two were ganging up on me, trying to weasel away the money that had just landed in my pocket. But it didn't really make any difference. I didn't think that would clean me out.

It was only when I felt the chill of the night that I realized I'd become dead drunk and was the only customer left.

"How much?" I asked.

"Four *yuan*," Uncle Ge Gen replied calmly.

"Four *yuan*? Can't be." I calculated in my head. I probably had three big cups of wine. That's twelve. I had two bowls of pork skin soup. That's four. The total should be sixteen *yuan*, which is what I laid on the greasy table.

"If I say four, it's four! I'm never wrong," Uncle Ge Gen became angry, taking four *yuan* from the pile of coins and shoving the rest into my pocket.

"Qiuxia, see him home. He's so drunk he can't even figure out his bill."

"No need. I can find my way home. She's . . ."

"Oh, she's my daughter."

I refused him over and over, but he insisted that his daughter see me home. Being familiar with his stubbornness, I had to give in. This girl couldn't have been more than sixteen or seventeen, and I had no idea what I could talk about with someone so young.

We walked through Ximending in the dead of night, dragging our long, lonely shadows behind us. After about fifteen minutes, she spoke up.

"Teacher, do you still live at the end of that alley off Linghou Street?"

"Teacher? Then you're . . . " A cold sweat broke out as the surprise sobered me up.

"You don't remember me? My name is Ge Qiuxia. I was in your sixth-grade class, the Xiao Class. The school year had barely started when you stopped coming. I was class leader, so Principal Lin and I went all over asking people where you'd gone before we heard that you'd been imprisoned. Didn't you get the towels, soap, toothbrush, and other things? Our classmates all chipped in to buy those for you."

Qiuxia spoke of the past in a sad tone, touching the scars in my heart. I let out a low moan. If she hadn't been there, I'm sure I'd have burst into tears.

"Now I remember. I certainly did receive the things you sent." In my mind, I continued to mumble, "Those things remained with me. Some were old and worn, but I didn't throw them away. I took them home with me when I was released from prison." I did not say this out loud.

"Sir, my dad says you really drink too much, and the work you do now is beneath you. You can't go on like this. You should find something else to do." Qiuxia spoke quietly, but her tone was firm and resolute.

"Find something else to do?" Stupefied, I stood there like a pigeon hit by an air rifle.

"That's right. People should earn a salary befitting their status. Take my dad, for example. He used to be a lowly artist, roaming around, and now he sells pork skin soup for a living. His conscience is clear with the money he earns. And me, I'm the daughter of a poor man. It's no disgrace for me to serve others to earn money. But you, sir, you're different. You should be aiming higher, not sinking so low. Sir, my dad says you can do better than this."

I saw the waxing moon through my tears, unable to say a word for a long time. After I parted with Qiuxia, I walked forward with purpose. Starting the next day, I wouldn't be going back to work as a janitor.

A Chance Encounter

It would be nearly three o'clock before Jian A-tao could rush to his home on Linghou Street in the old city on Saturday afternoons. He would leave a bundle of dirty clothes with his mother for his sister to wash before leaving again with a flurry of apologies. Then he would hurry over to the Southern Wind Tea House to drink a four-*yuan* cup of black tea. He had been teaching at the Liuguang Primary School in the remote Passing Through Village (Luguo Cun) by the Bazhang River. The name matched the reality for Passing Through Village, an infertile area on the belt of salt fields. Its roads were lined with emaciated willow trees and its wells only offered bitter, salty water, making anyone wish they could turn around and head straight back to where they came from. This was a village with no charm, little more than a minor stop one passed through in life.

A-tao did not go to the Southern Wind Tea House in order to meet people, nor was he hoping to find consolation there. The four-*yuan* cup of black tea was not sweet and did not have the slightest fragrance. Black tea in name only, it was really just sugar water.

Forlorn, A-tao's blank stare faced the bustling activity on what is called Tainan's Ginza while he drank his tea and drifted through old memories. A silent grief took hold as he thought of the wasted four years. The wounds left behind by more than a thousand days behind bars—every day, every scene, each with its own meaning and tenor—was etched on his mind.

To A-tao, a political prisoner who had just returned from a military prison, the confined, frightened society of the 1950s was inhumane. He had grown up here in the seat of the prefecture, had known many of the people, and was recognized by nearly half the city. But in those few months after his return, it was as though he was walking through a ghost town. The people he once knew were nowhere to be seen. He used to greet a dozen people on every block, sometimes stopping to have a short, pleasant chat with this or that acquaintance. But now, should these same acquaintances see him from afar, they would change direction and disappear down an alley, avoiding him like the devil. Some would fix him with a wide-eyed glare before striding away without a word, as though he were a leper. Sometimes he couldn't help it. If he ran into someone he thought of as a friend, he would call out a simple greeting, such as, "How've you been?" The friend's face would first turn white, then red, and then he would mutter something vague or an awkward "I'm good! Good!" before darting off like a shot.

There was no way A-tao could shed his glum feelings. He completely understood these people's selfishness, which stemmed from pressures that permeated an entire society that struggled in darkness. The brutal power of fascist rule had warped the people's minds, alienated them, and was now forcing them to live in mutual suspicion and fear.

Once A-tao had become used to the cold detachment and enmity, he stopped going out and spent all day inside with his books, thereby lessening the dread and unease inflicted on his friends.

Still, he couldn't spend all his days studying like a man of leisure. He had to earn a living. Nor could he continue to live off his frail, aging parents. That would be tantamount to giving them a slow death. Asking the elderly to share their limited food would be beyond cruel. He had tried to find work, but in the desolation of the 1950s, when even the most obedient and slavish people struggled to find work, a marked man like him could expect obstacles everywhere. For six months he worked as a casual laborer, operating a boiler at a water research institute. In the suffocating air between scalding hot boilers, he worked stripped down, covered in streams of sweat. Finally, he was fortunate to find a position in his former profession. After all, he'd once been a respected teacher at a primary school in the city.

A-tao whiled away close to two hours before he saw that the Du Xiaoyue snack shop next door would open soon. He was about to leave the tea house for a bowl of Du Xiaoyue's famous danzai noodles, as always, before heading home.

Just as he got up, through the tea house door he saw a tall, slim woman in a yellow dress, carrying a colorful parasol, saunter past. The delicate gold frames of her glasses and her pale moonlight complexion told him it was Lin Xuemei. He hesitated for only a moment before compulsively pushing through the door in pursuit. He was certain Xuemei would not reject him, as the others had, but he was not as confident that she would accept him with grace. After all, the bitter disagreements and misunderstandings between them were many, and he had broken her heart.

"Xuemei, how have you been?" A-tao called out to her quietly from behind. Stopping in surprise, she looked back. Her expression said that even in her dreams she'd never imagined running into him. They stood stock-still. Even the air between them seemed frozen. Finally, she forced a response: "You're back!" she said coldly, without a hint of emotion.

"I thought you were in Xingang. When did you get back to Tainan?"

A-tao spoke cautiously, afraid that any mention of Xingang would open old wounds. Sure enough, although her eyes were hidden behind glasses, she blinked rapidly, and a sparkling teardrop rolled down her face.

"I'm sorry!" His apology came quickly.

"It's really none of your business!" Xuemei's tone was steely, yet her icy manner quickly gave way to a gentler tone: "Want to talk?"

He led her back to the Southern Wind, where they found a quiet corner to sit. The potted yellow palm behind her was perfectly positioned to block the bright sunshine streaming in from the window, enveloping her in shadow. This brought back memories from the evening of his arrest. The agent responsible for the interrogation had stayed in the dark shadows while keeping a bright lamp pointed at him. Obviously, Lin Xuemei was now the interrogator and he was the accused.

"When did you get back? Why didn't you let me know?" she reproached him.

"I didn't want to bring you any trouble. And I worried you'd be sad when you saw me." He turned his head and let out a dry cough.

He thought of the impoverished post-war years. He and Lin Xuemei were a couple then, at least in the eyes of those around them. In reality, while they were together, not once had he raised matters of love and emotion. Lin Xuemei had regularly listened to outbursts of all the anger and indignation inside him. Full of enthusiasm, he had talked to her about things like Chen Yi's corrupt government, the events surrounding talks between the Kuomintang and the Communist Party, as well as the means by which the Taiwanese masses could be liberated again. Undoubtedly, Lin Xuemei confused the impassioned disclosure of his politics as a pretense for expressions of love. Was openly telling her of these extremely dangerous views that could easily lead to his execution not tantamount to an expression of wholehearted faith in her? Was this act of making her an insider not a confession of his love?

The truth is, anyone could have played this role for A-tao. Anyone willing to listen to his aspirations would have made him happy. Of course, nothing made him happier than having an intelligent, young woman like Lin Xuemei eagerly listen to him. He had never dreamed she would mistake his talk of politics for confessions of love.

Not once had he so much as touched her hand, nor had he paid any heed to her attractive figure or the ripe fruit of her soft, voluptuous breasts.

Six months or so later, Xuemei abruptly married a young doctor from Xingang. Not two weeks after their wedding, he was arrested with no word of his whereabouts. Soon came the terrible news that he had been executed as a traitor. Before A-tao could hurry over to offer his condolences, he too was arrested and began the three long years of life as a prisoner.

"So, you managed to make it out alive, but my older brother isn't home yet. He was charged under Article 5 and sentenced to twelve years," Xuemei said softly, and then took a sip of her cold tea.

"Your brother?" That came as a surprise to him.

"That's right! He used to talk about the same things you did, day in and day out. After that, while we were on our honeymoon, my husband spent every single day chattering about the same things that you had. I thought that all the young people of our generation were cast of the same die, that this was the spirit of our time! When I finally realized that you were actually a special group of people, it was already too late. I lost my husband, my brother . . . everything . . ."

Overwhelmed with shame, A-tao lowered his head, unable to offer her any comfort. Had they all been wrong? Beyond bringing misfortune to all those around them, had they achieved anything? Did their rallying and protesting for the dignity of their people bring about nothing but their own incarceration and the suffering of countless friends and family? When he walked on the street, all his acquaintances evaded him as though he were a leper. Could it be they were silently expressing their objections and contempt for them? No! No! History would restore justice to them. Even if temporary setbacks had occurred, the sacrifices made to fight for the Taiwanese people's political, economic, and social liberation would inevitably bear fruit in the future.

Xuemei, I am so sorry about what happened . . . I . . ." A-tao wanted to explain to her the grand ideals behind their thought and action, but he stopped. This was his same old speech. To a lonely, friendless young woman, it was nothing more than grandiose dreams that cut one off from life's realities.

"Then, what are you going to . . ." A-tao stammered.

Lin Xuemei's distressed and languishing face suddenly gave way to a faint smile.

"I'm going to find happiness," she said cheerfully, while opening her purse and taking out a black-and-white photograph.

"See here? This is my future husband. He works for a trading company in Kaohsiung."

A-tao picked up the photo and carefully examined each person in it. It was a family photo but missing a mother. At the center was a balding man in his fifties. He looked healthy and strong, but his freedom appeared to be restricted by the ill-fitting suit he wore. A girl and boy stood on either side of him. The boy appeared to be about ten years of age, in a primary school uniform. The girl was younger, possibly still be in kindergarten. Her happy smile showed the gaps in her teeth. Naturally, the man was holding his children close.

"You mean to say you're marrying the man in this photo?" Once again, A-tao was surprised. He carefully examined the balding man, who must have been twenty years her senior, old enough to be her father.

"That's right! He treats me really well!" Lin Xuemei smiled happily.

"But he has a son and daughter"

"Uh-huh. He lost his wife a year ago. Once we marry, I'll be a stepmother! I'll be nice to the children, just like a real mother."

"But you can do better than that, can't you?" As soon as he forced the question out of his mouth, he was filled with regret for such inappropriate words.

"Better? Really? Who else is going to marry me? Who would dare be with an unlucky woman whose husband was executed and brother arrested? He's the only one who doesn't care, opening his arms and offering me a warm embrace. I'm grateful and indebted to him. How is this not better?"

Xuemei spoke calmly, but he saw the hot tears gathering in the corners of her eyes before they rolled down her cheeks, one after the other.

"Xuemei, if your wedding hasn't been finalized yet, please give it some more thought. Why not marry me? I'd do everything possible to make you happy."

He finally said it. Representing all those who had hurt her, he wanted to make it up to her. Although he didn't really love her, marriage is not dependent upon the existence of love, and undoubtedly includes many complicated factors. Who could say that their union would be destined for failure?

"If this is your way of proposing, it's too late."

Lin Xuemei glanced at him dejectedly while she carefully returned the photograph to her purse and stood up coldly. I have to go. I'm afraid we won't have another opportunity to meet. Take care, A-tao!"

Unwilling to explain why she would not accept his marriage proposal, Lin Xuemei walked out with her head down. Jian A-tao stared at her retreating figure, suddenly feeling that her resolute departure concealed a hopeless frailty and a hint of hesitation, but he weakly remained seated in his chair, not daring to stand up and stop her, not willing to engage in another struggle.

He got up and walked out of Southern Wind Tea House. She was nowhere in sight. Forgetting to go to Du Xiaoyue for his danzai noodles, he slowly walked home.

The Interrogation

1

It was a late autumn morning. Although the leaden sky still hung heavy, and the wind brought a chill, Jian A-tao's life did not diverge one bit from his routine. He left home at 6:30, taking the number 10 bus to a stop in front of an abandoned brick kiln. He then walked the last twenty minutes to the primary school.

His first class started at 8:40. Just like Pavlov's dog, on hearing the bell, he would tuck his textbook under his arm and go to class. He was not exactly happy, but he wasn't feeling down either. He just appeared a bit dejected as he went off to do his job.

After arriving in the class, putting the textbook on his desk, and clearing his throat, just as he was about to begin his opening remarks to get the students' attention, Old Zhang, the janitor, arrived at the classroom door. "Mr. Jian, the principal would like to see you in his office," Zhang said in his thick Shandong accent.

"What could be so urgent? I was just about to start the lecture," A-tao grumbled. He was annoyed but did not dare to keep the principal waiting. He instructed the students to read through the passage and followed Old Zhang.

He was instantly aware of a somber atmosphere when he stepped into the principal's office. Both bald-headed Principal Wang and the director of human resources, Lin Wenchong, were present. His arrival brought awkward expressions to their faces. There was also a stranger in the office with them, a thin, short man in his thirties. He remained expressionless but had a cultured and amicable air about him, not the look of a manual laborer.

"This is Mr. Jian A-tao," Principal Wang reluctantly forced out the words as he pointed toward A-tao.

The stranger offered no greeting and merely examined him with a careful stare as though he was identifying Jian A-tao with a mental image. He quietly waited for the stranger to begin speaking, but the man remained silent as he pulled a document from his pocket.

"Once you've read this, we can leave." the stranger said pointedly. A-tao took the document. As soon as he saw the large red stamp of the

Garrison Command, he had a good idea of what was to come. It was an arrest warrant, demanding that he appear for questioning. The document did not indicate what kind of case it was all about, but A-tao had a pretty good idea. He nodded in consent, knowing that this misfortune was likely connected to the arrest of his good friend, Gan Huoshun, a month earlier.

Principal Wang and Director Lin were staring at him with worried looks, but there was nothing they could say before a secret service agent. Fear and caution kept them quiet, terrified to say another word.

"Walk ahead of me!" the agent said. A-tao walked in front, looking at the familiar mahogany trees that were so full of life. They proceeded from the doorway to the school gate in front of the statue of Sun Yat-sen, where a Ford sedan was parked.

He sat in the back with the agent as the driver started the car. They drove across the rank Zuochang Stream, through Zuochang Township, and headed for K City. But they did not go directly to their destination. They turned up one street and down another in O City before finally coming to a stop in front of a three-story Western-style building in a narrow alleyway. Obviously, the agent did not want him knowing the location of this building, so they had taken a roundabout way of getting there. In fact, there was no need for that, as Jian A-tao seldom ventured out and did not know his way around O City at all. Even north, south, east, and west were a puzzle to him.

The agent motioned for him to step out of the car and walk in front, as he had before, to ensure that he would not try to run. They went up to a room on third floor, and as soon as the door opened, A-tao was petrified. Three rows of desks were crammed into a room of no more than 700 square feet, and there must have been at least thirty people squeezed in. There was nothing on the desktops, and these people were not working. They were engaged in animated discussions, drinking tea, reading newspapers, smoking, and killing time. Still, one thing set this office apart from other offices. On a few of the desks, he saw shiny pairs of handcuffs.

The agent greeted a few of the people inside. It seemed that all he did was chitchat with someone in the corner before they headed back out. A-tao had assumed that this was their destination, but he was mistaken. He could not imagine why the agent had brought him here just to hang out for a bit before leaving again. However, these things were not for him to question. He could only follow along like a sheep.

Next, they drove across the Ai River before stopping in front of another building. A-tao silently made his way up the stairs. The polished terrazzo staircase was wide enough for three or four people side by side. As he climbed the stairs, he saw rough-looking men dressed like thugs and gangsters, and women with lips painted an exaggerated blood-red, wearing wild and flamboyant clothes. These men and women appeared to belong to the lower rungs of society, people who made a living through unsavory business. As they reached the fourth floor, realization suddenly hit him that the building was a brothel. He had heard about them, but as he had never been in the area, it hadn't been clear to him. He could not understand why the Garrison Command would have offices above a brothel. Perhaps it allowed easy access to informers.

The agent knocked on a door, which was immediately opened by someone inside. The rooms were arranged like a standard apartment, with all the requirements—living room, bedrooms, sitting room, and kitchen, taking up about a thousand square feet of living space. The furnishings in all the rooms were like an ordinary household. In the living room, the sofa and coffee table were outdated and had a somewhat moldy smell.

A-tao sat on the sofa and waited. The agent who had brought him had apparently left, as he was no longer anywhere to be seen.

Languishing in the tedium, A-tao closed his eyes, letting his mind drift into a haziness. Soon his stomach began to rumble, and the intensity of his nervousness increased as the urge to urinate grew stronger and stronger. He stood up.

"Stay where you are!" A big burly man had appeared out of nowhere and rushed over, pressed him heavily by his shoulders back down on the sofa. A-tao realized the severity of his situation at that moment. He was under arrest, and his movements were under their control.

"I just want to go to the toilet." A-tao protested.

"You have to ask permission to go anywhere. Understand?"

The agent sounded impatient, but still took him to the toilet rather than leave him in discomfort. As he faced the filthy yellowed urinal, tears rolled down A-tao's cheeks as he thought of his infant son, wailing for his mother's milk. If he didn't return today, or if he never returned, who would raise the child? In this age, everyone was afraid for their own lives. Who would dare to lift a hand to help his wife and son through difficulties when they might be implicated in a rebellion? As a living example, his own experiences could be a lesson for others. He had been good friends with Gan Huoshun for many years, with a friendship that dated back to the end of the war. Then Gan was arrested for participating in an armed rebellion. For violating Article 5 of The Punishment of Rebellion Act, he was sentenced to twelve years in prison. A year later, Jian A-tao was also arrested. However, he was only sentenced to five years imprisonment under Article 9 of the Anti-Espionage Regulations for failing to report. Although Gan Huoshun may have been acting under Cai Xiaoqian, leader of the Taiwanese Communist Party's Provincial Work Committee, A-tao was certainly not. In 1945, A-tao had been arrested after coming into contact with a schoolmate from middle school named Wu Duoxing. Unfortunately, Wu was the brains behind the entire organization and the new leader of the Taiwanese Communist Party. After this, no manner of explanation could absolve Jian A-tao, who was wrongly imprisoned for more than three years. Then an amnesty was announced, including pardons for those charged with the political crime of concealing information, and he was fortunate enough to be released. His case was entirely different and completely unrelated to that of Gan Huoshun. A-tao knew that Gan was a fervent Marxist. He believed in the myth of the dictatorship of the proletariat, referring to the ideology as scientific socialism. He was obsessed by his beliefs and had long since become a dogmatist. A-tao was a socialist, but his idea of utopia was something like the welfare states of Sweden and Denmark. He could also be considered a liberal, not in the old sense of liberalism of Hu Shih, but in the new sense, which had been tested and changed by Marxism. Therefore, he found the idea of fascist dictatorship to be repugnant and understandably also disliked the so-called dictatorship of the proletariat.

Ideological differences had no bearing on their friendship. They had come of age in the same place and time. Despite their inability to agree on ideology, they had plenty of mutual interests, including their views on literature and life. Gan Huoshun was released after serving his full twelve-year sentence. A-tao had no reason to avoid him, but he remained guarded and seldom visited him. Within any year, aside from seeing his old friend with gifts during the Dragon Boat Festival, Mid-Autumn Festival and Lunar New Year, he would only visit Gan on rare occasions for urgent matters. In this time of peril, for those branded as former political prisoners to engage in regular interaction would be inviting disaster. Big Brother was always watching and would not be pleased to see former political prisoners enjoying each other's company. Such a friendship would be a step toward reorganization. In the vigilant eye of Big Brother, there was no room for this charade of licking one another's old scars, scars that had been produced by Big Brother's own hand.

About a month earlier A-tao had heard of Gan Huoshun's arrest. He did not know if Gan had been involved in secretive activities since his release, but he himself had walked the straight and narrow. He thought that, regardless of what Gan had been arrested for this time, it was in no way related to him. As an old friend, he was duty bound to visit his family, which was nothing unusual. Even if he was unable to help, at least he could be there to comfort his old friend's wife and child.

He could not have known that such a move was a mistake. Big brother would not overlook even this minor detail. When A-tao arrived at Gan's home, he didn't even have time to greet Huoshun's wife before he was seized by a hulking secret agent who had been inside lying in wait for just such an opportunity. A-tao had walked into a trap.

But the agent merely recorded his name, address, and place of employment, before letting him go. Of course, he had Huoshun's wife confirm these details. Once the information A-tao gave had been verified, he was released with a smile.

A-tao knew this was only the beginning of his nightmare. Big Brother would not let it go at that. He mentally prepared himself but had no way of knowing when his arrest would occur, nor where nor how.

2

"Bring in the suspect!" A voice thundered from behind the tightly closed door across from Jian A-tao. The agent who had just taken him to the toilet gave him a shove, signaling him to enter the room. As he dragged his reluctant feet toward the door, it flew halfway open; he was pulled in and then the door shut behind him.

"Sit over there!"

A short, middle-aged man bulging with fat, like the Laughing Buddha, spoke Mandarin with a Jiangsu accent. His legs were so short he looked like a rolling ball when he walked. A-tao made a quick assessment of his surroundings. There were two other agents in this bedroom of about 250 or 300 square feet. One was tall, the other short, like the black and white Gods of Impermanence that take the dead to the underworld. Lazily sitting on the spring bed, they watched his every move.

A-tao and the buddha took seats across from each other at a desk.

With an unhappy look, the buddha spread out a thin twenty-line sheet of paper and lowered his head to write with a ballpoint pen. A-tao looked at his short, childlike hands, covered in little dimples.

"What's your name? When were you born? Where do you live? Your job? Where is your family from?" The buddha spoke loudly and clearly, firing one question after another.

A-tao was familiar with the routine. He used his Taiwanese-accented Mandarin to respond to each of the questions. When he replied that he was a native of Tainan City in the Province of Taiwan, the buddha paused for a moment. A-tao knew that the buddha had thought him to be an old "taro," a mainlander, because he had the buzzcut of an old taro.

"Have you ever committed a crime?" The buddha's questions had gradually turned to more serious matters.

"Yes, I have. Under the Anti-Espionage Regulations, I was sentenced to five years imprisonment." The buddha was visibly shocked and confused.

"What did you say you were convicted of?" The buddha could not recall what these Regulations signified.

"Concealing information!"

"Ah, yes. I see!" The buddha relaxed a bit. With a face covered in sweat, he mumbled the words "concealing information," then continued writing down A-tao's statement.

"But I was released after three years," A-tao added. This was another surprise for the buddha, who stared blankly again, not believing that a political prisoner could be released early.

"Why was that?"

"I guess it was an amnesty. I'm not sure myself."

"Amnesty? What's an amnesty?"

The buddha pulled out a dirty handkerchief to wipe his sweaty forehead and pushed a sheet of old newspaper over so A-tao could write down "amnesty." he complied.

"Oh, that's it! I see." The buddha looked as though he'd been given a treasure, as he carefully copied the characters into the statement.

"Since you were a political prisoner, you must be in the same cohort as Gan Huoshun? What's your relationship to him? Tell me the truth!" The buddha switched to a more threatening demeanor.

"My crime of twenty years ago had absolutely nothing to do with Gan Huoshun's case. I'm not at liberty to disclose the details. When I was locked up by the Counterintelligence Bureau, they made me swear I wouldn't reveal them to anyone. You're from the Garrison Command, not the Counterintelligence Bureau, so please contact them if you need to know anything about it." A-tao employed his right to silence.

"Don't give me that shit! The secret police is us and we're the secret police." The frustrated buddha was losing his composure. But then he didn't pursue the matter.

"You said you were released twenty years ago. Then you've been free for twenty, right?"

"Right. Gan Huoshun was released five or six years ago, so the two of us have only been back in contact for two or three years now."

"Oh! Then it looks like you two are pretty close?" With a sly smile, the buddha finally grabbed hold of something he could use."

"Not at all! I'm busy teaching at the primary school, I've only had time to visit him a few times a year. It seems that his crime is related to the Taiwanese Communist Party, but I have no connection to that! I was dragged into it because of a friend."

"You're not in the TCP, so you must be for Taiwan independence." The buddha grinned as he drilled him.

"I believe in the Three Principles of the People, all right?" A-tao could not stop himself from provoking the man with a little retort.

"How dare you!" The buddha slapped the table as his face flushed bright red: "If you insist on being arrogant and rude, then we don't need to drag this on any longer. You can be taken straight to Taipei!"

"Yeah! Yeah! This guy's so pig-headed, you shouldn't show him any mercy. Let's give him a beating and send him to Taipei!"

The Gods of Impermanence, who had been lounging on the bed, stood up in a violent fit. They put on a worthy show of curses and accusations, concluding with: "Commie spies like this should be executed. What are we keeping him around for?"

A-tao was more than familiar with this kind of interrogation. They would play the good cop, bad cop routine. One would try to intimidate the prisoner while the other would act sweet and pretend to offer support, hoping he'd give what they were after.

"Don't worry about it. It probably wasn't on purpose!" The buddha had taken on the role of the good cop to keep the interrogation rolling.

"What did you talk about when you visited Gan Huoshun?"

"Quite a bit! We talked about things like the tropical fish his family is raising and selling to make some money. His wife had recently had surgery."

"Bullshit! I mean did you and Gan Huoshun talk about things like how corrupt this government is? Or that the commies are going to attack Taiwan from the mainland, so we have to prepare to meet them on their arrival and make plans to help the commie bandits overthrow the government . . ."

"I never heard anything like that!" Jian A-tao remained calm and composed.

"Don't think we don't know about you two colluding and plotting together. If you're still not willing to tell the truth and keep avoiding the topic, we'll be forced to resort to torture!" the buddha shouted grimly as he pointed a finger at A-tao's forehead.

The Gods of Impermanence were spoiling for a fight and had awaited just such an opportunity. In a flash they were standing on either side of him, holding his shoulders and pressing between them. A-tao felt pain radiate out as their fingernails dug into his shoulders.

"Aha! You'd better be careful now. Now tell us, did he give you any publications to read?"

"Yes! Yes, he did!" A-tao quickly responded.

Seeing that he was willing to cooperate and respond, the Gods of Impermanence relaxed their grip and returned to the bed to sit down.

"What books did he give you?"

"A few old issues of *Taiwan Political Review* and *The China Journal*," A-tao explained. "*Taiwan Political Review* is published by Kang Ningxiang, and your own Party's Hu Qiuyuan publishes *The China Journal*, both approved by the government. They're legal!"

"Ha! Well!" The buddha's face strained in a grimace, as though he had something difficult on his mind. "These magazines are bad news from cover to cover! You buy them regularly?"

"No! I can't afford to. They were old issues that Gan Huoshun didn't want anymore."

"All right, all right. Let's not talk about magazines. Did he give you any other books?"

"I really enjoy the study of Taiwanese literature, so he once bought Ozaki Hideki's *A Study of Literature in the Former Colonies* and brought it back from Japan for me. I paid him for the book. He didn't just give it to me."

"What's this 'Taiwanese literature?' And what's this 'literature in the former colonies?' You've got more than enough to eat and nothing to do, so you spend your time on these ridiculous things?"

The buddha had had enough. It was like A-tao was killing him with all these impossible-to-understand new terms. He had a splitting headache and was sinking into a terrible bout of confusion and worry as he tried to understand.

"Is there anything else you want to talk about?" The buddha was clearly at his wit's end trying to get the answers he wanted and was ready to end the interrogation.

The buddha quickly finished writing up the statement and told A-tao to read it. He found numerous incorrect characters on what looked more like an interview with its question and response style. But these errors were none of his concern. As he added his signature and thumbprint to the bottom of the document, he was laughing to himself.

The buddha also pulled out a professionally printed piece of paper and asked him to sign that as well. At the top of the page, it was written that divulging any aspect of the interrogation was strictly forbidden and would result in legal action. A-tao was left wondering exactly what law he would break were he to tell others about today's events.

The buddha was overly affable as he walked him to the door, feeling unburdened from this heavy responsibility. He even politely opened the door to see him out.

As they parted, the buddha was all smiles. With utmost respect he implored, "Should you have forgotten to mention anything, please come straight back to tell us. At your convenience!"

Ah-tao did not know whether to laugh or cry over that and wondered about the buddha's mental stability.

He rushed outside and glanced at his watch. It was 11:30. If he hurried back to the school, he would still have time for lunch.

3

RED DRAGONFLY

Lay Chih-ying
(translated by Darryl Sterk)

> Why am I unable to bear loneliness? Am I sad over my unfilled youth? Why do I feel this spiritual emptiness? My hand, resting by the window, feels almost incapacitated, as my vision begins to blur . . .
> —Lü Heruo, "Autumn of Clarity"

I cut into your arm. Your skin is as crisp as paper, but blotchy as well. The dark brown birthmark on your wrist is impossible to miss. How could I not recognize you?

I follow the brachial vein toward your palm, where a network of vessels and nerves gets more and more convoluted. I remember you used to complain that your hand might be short a few tendons, or why else did you play the piano so clumsily for Lü san during your lessons?

At dusk back then we often went to the Taipei First Girls High School, where Lü san was teaching. He would be waiting at the gate to take us to the music room. You'd met Lü san before I came to Taipei for high school, when he was your music teacher. I asked you how you got acquainted. You mentioned something about him taking you to some gathering. You would fill me in when the time was right. I should just focus on my studies. After sitting in on several of your lessons, I started longing for the approach of summer, because the closer summer came, the later night would fall and the longer your lessons would last, which would afford me more of those rare moments to observe you without awkwardness. The tall windows in the classroom sometimes seemed to stretch taller in the angling light of dusk, which shone on your back. You and Lü san would be going at it, battling against the squiggly notes on the sheet music, while I just sat there, not doing a thing, feeling jealous that the early evening light could creep in and caress your hips, your back, your elbow, your sweaty brow. Sometimes you would practice a piece so long you both gave up, and Lü-san would teach you how to sing. He had studied in Japan, and had even held a solo recital in the public auditorium. I would always hum along on the sly. Lü san said you had a good voice. Pity that you were so intent on playing the piano and didn't take singing seriously. I actually didn't care how you played. All I cared about was the feeling I had sitting entranced in a corner of that classroom, listening to the intermittent alternation of the piano and your conversation. The choppy notes when you played badly were themselves a kind of beauty, like the falling leaves outside the window.

Before I cut open your hand I give your palm a secret, secret squeeze, but no force flows out of your palm in return. The formaldehyde masks my tears. The eyes and noses of all my classmates are all smarting, too, and all just as red as mine.

The force of your grip last enveloped my palm in early March, two years after the Retrocession. In those days we had to run down alleys to avoid the military police, sometimes even duck into a gutter. Some days

Red Dragonfly

it took us over an hour to negotiate the short distance from our rented room on Gutingding to the school. You would grip my hand hard as we sprinted the final stretch, a mere hundred and fifty meters from the Office of the Governor General, from where he looked down on the chaos all around. We half-closed our eyes, not wishing to see any blood, but we couldn't miss the expressions of panic or rage on the faces of the people along the way. I placed my faith in your hand, wherever it led. Finally, I realized that the school gatekeeper was motioning for us to hurry in, and then the gate slammed shut, punctuating the commotion outside with darkness and silence. You leaned against the gate, breathless, and thanked the fellow in the booth in Japanese. You were still holding my hand tightly, your palm moist and hot. I was too embarrassed to wriggle free, just watched the sweat on your chest paint a splash-ink Chinese mountain and stream landscape on your shirt.

I remember one time Lü san tapped your broad chest and said, "You have a beautiful singing voice hidden in here." I'd really like to dig it out, like a miner. Now I'm helping Lü san fulfill his wish to excavate your voice, by cutting open your chest, now so thin that all the ribs are starkly visible. I pull at the pectoralis muscle, slicing it away from your ribs. But the music to "Red Dragonfly" does not come pouring out, nor the petals of "Sakura." All that emerges is the stench that has yet to be masked by formaldehyde. We all knit our brows like rescuers at the mouth of a collapsed mine, pulling out the twisted corpses one after another, except that all I pull out now is your heart muscle. The lobes of your lungs, which should have shrivelled, are full of fluid. I pop the dissection needle in, and a foul fluid squirts out of the little hole. Even an abandoned mine has an echo, but now your chest is a germ-filled pond. Something dawns on me. I think I hear your struggle and cannot stop the tears from blurring my vision, but I can blame that on the formaldehyde too.

I remember when I first arrived in Taipei. You took me everywhere, including to the bench by the lotus pond at New Park. So many red dragonflies were dancing on the water under a clear sky. On a whim you softly sang words from a Japanese folksong:

> *Like a fire in the western sky, red dragonfly!*
> *On what day did I see you last . . .*

The faint vibration of resonance passed through your chest cavity, then to your backbone, and through the back of the bench on which we were sitting, hitting me like a wave. In the lingering notes of your singing voice, I was a docile subject, a dim star under the moon.

"Japanese dogs! Pftt!" shouted an armed Chinese, killing the dreaminess. Stunned by his savage appearance, we spent a while trying to figure out just what it was he said in his thick hometown accent. On one of the frightful days that followed in early March I saw a panicky face covered in blood near the park begging for help. In that confused moment I had no way to offer anyone sympathy, let alone help. Later, I was pretty sure it was the same mainlander who had called us Japanese dogs, and wish I'd taken him to the hospital.

I slash at your intestines. The mesentary has stiffened, with a small patch of ugly yellow fat attached. I slice open your stomach. I can make out the contents of your last meal: a few strips of blackened vegetables and a clump of what must be rice gruel.

Yesterday, when I walked home to our rented room in Gutingding, as usual, I took the long way round to avoid the noodle stand at the end of the alley. That was our "kitchen," where we used to eat for lack of other options. Now I can't stomach the emptiness on the other side of the table or the lady who runs the stand's courteous inquiry, "Where's your cousin? When'll he be back?" Initially I told her you'd gone down south to take care of your sick mother, but whenever I tried to forget you, her question forced me to confront the brutal fact of your nonexistence. In the end, I decided to skirt the area, wanting to avoid eye contact with her, even if it meant going hungry. I imagine she's guessed what has happened to you by now. Lately people have grown fearful, worried about loved ones who disappeared in the night. On winter nights, through the screen window of our *washitsu*, I can see smoke rising from the noodle stand. I often shed solitary tears at the imagery of warmth.

Your mom, my aunt, really is sick. After you went missing, she knelt daily in front of the altar, praying to the Buddha and the ancestors for your protection. She often knelt until she fell asleep and crumpled to the side. When a family member woke her up, she went back to praying. In the end, everyone felt it best to put a blanket over her instead of waking her. One time she wasn't sleeping. She'd had a stroke. They only found out by the smell after she'd lost control of her bowels. The last time I went to see her, we could only communicate through our tears. I told her not to worry so much. What else could I do?

In the days before you were taken away, my course load at the School of Medicine got heavier, and I seldom accompanied you to the school to see Lü san. But when you got home, it was always Lü san said this or that. We were supposed to be practicing Chinese, but you'd get too excited for that and switch back into Japanese. You gave me copies of a few stories Lü san had written, saying we could translate them into Chinese for practice. You told me that he and a few Mainland writers, like Lu Xun and Guo Moruo, were "top-notch." We had to help translate Lü san's Japanese stories into Mandarin "before the day came," you said, to introduce him to our compatriots. Spittle flew as you talked, and you urged me to model myself on the doctor in the short story "Autumn of Clarity," to adopt his humanitarian ethos. I didn't want to spoil your mood. I'd only heard a little about the writers from China you mentioned, but I could sense from the excitement in your voice an indescribable sense of high expectations. I didn't quite understand your "before the day came." Under the lamp your Adam's apple cut a lovely silhouette that rose and fell to the rhythm of your speech. It was a dance for your Adam's apple, a shadow puppet play for voice control.

Yes, now I've begun slicing into your neck. The veins are empty and deathly gray. I've made a point of cutting open your windpipe and hunting for your vocal cords, once the source of emotional highs, now silently inlaid in your windpipe, like two sprouts withered before they had the chance to grow. Your stubble pokes the back of my hand. I wonder how long since you last shaved. Not since you were torn away from me in the dead of night?

That night, we were woken from our dreams by the muffled sound of knocking at the door. You awoke immediately. I thought it was the landlord until someone called your name gruffly, louder and louder, closer and closer. You jumped up to get dressed. A breeze blew by my cheek when you lifted up the blanket. Panicking, I sat up. The door to our room burst open and two cops stormed in, followed by our sleepy-eyed landlord. They wanted to take you away. I asked them why, and they said they were taking you to the station for a chat. Their vicious faces made it clear there'd be no chat.

By then, you were dressed. You told me not to worry, that you'd be right back. As I watched you walk down the hallway, my emotions burst forth and I ran toward you. At the sound of my footsteps, you looked back and broke free. We held each other tightly, pressing our bodies together. Your stubbly cheek against mine smarted, but I didn't want to let you go. Finally the police jerked us away from each other, pulled us apart.

My face turned red and puffy, and stayed that way until one summer evening a few months later at dusk. I felt quite happy at first, but then, when I saw white smoke rising from the end of the alley, I knew that you had said farewell.

Later I, too, was taken to the police station for questioning. But I had no answers for them, because I really didn't know what you and Lü-san were up to. I even sneaked over to the high school to seek him out, but the gatekeeper said he'd quit his job, and I didn't know whom in Taipei you were in touch with, except me.

Now that we've been reunited, I've looked forward every day to our regular meetings, twice a week. Afterward, I make my solitary way home, walking down alleys and crossing through the field, where I see clouds of red dragonflies.

> *Like a fire in the western sky, red dragonfly!*
> *Resting on the tip of a fishing pole*

I hum that sentimental folksong in mourning for those days when we crossed the field, shoulder to shoulder.

I approach our semiweekly meeting with dread, because after every time I turn you over, looking here and there, I am unable to sleep at night. I try not to sleep, actually, because I don't want you to appear in my dreams all cut up. I am afraid you'll ask me to stop dissecting you, even though I promised you that when I was done I'd sew you back up, and you'd be whole again, the same as you used to be. Later, when I realized the improbability of making you whole, I felt deeply guilty. I thought at first I could treat you better than anyone else, that I'd totally possess you, and I refused to switch to another cadaver. But I ended up leaving you in pieces.

Luckily, I've seen you only once in my dreams. You were facing away from me, looking at the field we crossed to get to the school, and what I smelled was not pungent formaldehyde but, faintly, your sweat. You didn't turn around, but from your sharply protruding scapula I recognized your broad, thickset back. Thinking of how pathetically thin and bony it has become, I murmured, "I'm sorry, I have to finish my studies." In the end, I told myself that what I had seen in my dream wasn't you, but a shell you'd cast off, like the molted skin of a dragonfly nymph poised on a stalk of rice straw. The real you was flying freely, like a dragonfly somewhere on the horizon.

Next I cut into your ankle with a scalpel. There's a band of tendon there, like the protector of some secret. I see the greenish purple of your ankle and calf, and the clumps of torn skin. I don't even want to think what heavy, rusted instrument of torture was wrapped around your ankles to cut into them like that.

I am reminded of the abandoned house at the end of a lane on the busiest street back home, the one the kids called the haunted house. Once, in junior high, you took me there to explore. Banyan trees straddling the wall had thrust their aerial roots into the house, where they found purchase and thickened, getting bigger and bigger, until in the end they would bring the house down.

You took me to see a little mound of dirt in the courtyard of that Western-style house and told me a secret. The wandering minstrel who performed on occasion in the village when we were young had buried his little monkey here. Not long before, you'd seen him in the neighborhood, seemingly afraid someone would spot him. The brim of his hat pulled low, he turned into that house, and you followed him into the courtyard and hid behind the wall, watching his every move. First he sat down and talked to the mound. Then he indulged in "self-abuse" upon it, and his howls and groans made you think he was a man possessed. You cried out despite yourself.

He saw you, told you not to be afraid, and explained that the mound was for his old pal the monkey. Back in the day, it and his handler had performed together for the first time in this courtyard, and now the house had been abandoned, leaving him alone. He once spent the night in the house after performing in the village. Feeling the urge, he just had to "self-abuse," and his monkey started to imitate him. Once the monkey had started, it couldn't stop. That night, its vital energy spent, it died. Devastated, the man buried his monkey in the courtyard. Every year on the anniversary of its demise the man would return to sprinkle his seed as an offering.

I didn't know what you were talking about. What was "self-abuse"? His "seed"? Half joking, you laughed and said, "Cousin, I'll show you." You held me from behind; I tried to wriggle free until, at the touch of our cheeks, I succumbed to the warmth of your body and the smell of your sweat when our cheeks touched. I was like a pale puppet, speechless. For a moment, all I heard was the sound of your breathing. You reached into my pants and held me tight. When you started rubbing me, I felt a tingling. I thought I was going to piss my pants. I cried for you to stop, but you wouldn't, you were having too good a time. A sticky white liquid shot out, giving me quite a shock. "You're a man now," you said. "But remember to control yourself. Don't be like that monkey." That was our secret rite of passage.

I returned home recently and walked alone to the haunted house. Now completely overtaken by banyan trees, it's even eerier and gloomier than before. Facing the forbidding shadows of the trees and the mound, I started rubbing myself and wailing like a lonely ghost, my brief ecstacy mingled with suppressed sadness spilling onto the mound. If someone had happened by, it would have made quite a story.

I regard your shriveled penis, now completely black. I cut away the scrotum and, after a careful inspection, while my classmates are taking a break, I pop the testes into my pocket—a crypt for unborn offspring who died before tasting victory. Now they're mine.

Finally, we are going to dissect your skull. I ask my classmate to flay the skin of your face, while I excuse myself for a bathroom break, because I cannot look calmly at your face.

When I return, I tell myself that the gory visage doesn't belong to you. Once again I take up the scalpel and slice away your prim lips, to study the inside of your mouth. Then we pry your skull open to carve away your hardened brain. You do not bleed or struggle. Without a whimper you meekly allow us to cut it out. That's when I lose control. My partner pulls me away, assuming I'm exhausted. Since the beginning of the term, I've been the one who insisted on wielding the scalpel, which upsets my partner, who takes the opportunity to try to take over. I don't let him. You're all mine.

But I can't make another cut. I pick up the discarded mask of your face and inspect it carefully. Yes, there's an angle at the end of each of your eyebrows, a scar on the right, and pitted skin from eczema under the stubble. It's you, it really is you, but you've gotten so thin. The shape of your sunken cheeks pains me when I compare it to the full, ample flesh I remember. Are you willing to be reborn in me? I ask you softly. Do you want to feel the breath of life through me? I thrust my finger deep into where your mouth would be, and your lips seem to softly close upon it, as if to say, "Yes, I'm willing." And so I endure the sting of the formaldehyde and lay your face over mine. What a searing pain! I can't keep my eyes open, but I can feel all the eyes in the room on me.

The teacher rushes over, awards me a slap, and as a bonus cries *"Bakayaro!"*—stupid bastard. His teaching assistant drags me out of the classroom to the sink to rinse my face. My cheeks once again swell red, but in my heart the warmth of happiness wells up. The warm current takes me back to that afternoon in the haunted house and to the night when we parted. In the moment when the professor tore your face skin off me, I wished the cadaver on the table was one of those cops or the teacher who tore us apart. I would happily dissect either of them. Cousin, oh cousin! We never knew that the lyrics of the Japanese folksong would be prophetic.

On what day did I see you last? On the day I lifted the sheet in the dissection lab for human anatomy class.

4

AUNTIE TIGER

Li Ang
(translated by Jewel Lo and Dafydd Fell)

1

On August 14, 1945, Japan surrendered, bringing an end to World War II and the war in the Pacific. It marked the start of a new and complex era for the residents of Taiwan. Leaving behind a full fifty years of Japanese colonial rule, they looked forward to returning to China, their motherland.

Japanese colonial rule came to an end and was replaced by the Kuomintang (KMT) regime from China. In the initial period, a diverse range of Chinese political forces, including leftist and rightist groups, flocked to the island.

In Taichung city, while right-wing intellectuals were busy organizing a Preparatory Committee to Welcome the National Government, Xie Xuehong clearly had no expectations of the KMT regime whatsoever. In

September 1945, a month before the National Government sent Chen Yi to Taiwan to establish the Taiwan Administrative Executive Office, Xie organized a "Taiwan People's Association Preparatory Meeting."

The association's goal was to call on everyone on the island to unite in a struggle for democracy. Most of the participants had been anti-Japanese fighters in the colonial era, and many had been imprisoned for as long as a decade or more. Together with progressives from all over, they started by organizing the masses.

On September 30, the association convened a people's assembly at its first meeting in the Taichung Theater, formally establishing it later at the Da Hua Restaurant. The association proposed items such as: implementing an 8-hour work system, safeguarding people's freedom, mediating their disputes, and preventing Japanese soldiers from inciting aboriginals to riot. Enjoying widespread support, the association established branches all over Taiwan.

Xie Xuehong not only participated in the establishment of the People's Association but also helped organize the Taiwanese Federation of Labor and the Taiwan Farmers' Association and looked forward to linking up with student groups.

In addition, she sought the support of KMT journalists and infiltrated the KMT army newspaper, *Peace Daily* (originally called *Mopping-up News*), with her people. Almost all the new hires of editors, reporters, copy editors, and managers were recommended by Xie Xuehong. Under her control, *Peace Daily*'s circulation rapidly increased to more than 10,000, second only to the largest paper in Taipei, *Taiwan Shin Sheng Daily News*.

Between the Japanese surrender in late 1945 and the outbreak of the February 28 Incident in 1947, Xie lived above the Da Hua Restaurant, which was run by her brother, Xie Zhennan.

Xie's younger brother had changed the last character of his name to one with the same sound but a different meaning from "boy/man" to "south." "My father had wanted a boy," Xie commented, "but then I came along, so he named me Jianü, meaning fake girl. Later when he got the son he'd hoped for, he named him Zhennan, meaning real boy."

Were "fake girl" and "real boy" just changes in the form of address? Was the Da Hua Restaurant an ordinary restaurant or, at a different time and place, might it have provided bar girl services?

Whatever the reason, Xie Xuehong was denounced and criticized on both sides of the Taiwan Strait owing to her association with the Da Hua Restaurant. The Chinese Communist Party claimed that while running the restaurant she was guilty of many unspeakable things, that she led such a sullied life that she was no longer qualified to be a communist.

In Taiwan, the KMT regime also insulted her with lines like "Wakened up from a 30-year red dynasty dream, only to earn the epithets of bar girl and deserter."

When she lived above the Da Hua Restaurant, all sorts of people who met her there described her as "friendly and plainly dressed in a faded qipao, no different from any other woman."

At that time people commonly called women forty-five and older, "Obasan."

In Japanese, "obasan" is a general term for women of low social status; in Taiwan, it became a common form of address for older women. Nonetheless, it was reserved for Xie Xuehong. When someone in her circle mentioned "Obasan," everyone knew it meant her and not just any elderly woman, for it indicated respect for her experience, seniority, and morals. It became an honorific: "The Taiwanese Obasan."

However, when she mingled with top officials and high society, she was heavily made up and wore diamonds and gold rings. Dressed in silk qipaos, with gold necklaces and diamond rings, she was described by younger revolutionary male comrades in these terms:

"During this time, Xie Xuehong actively socialized with influential officials. Making use of her experience, charming manners, and remarkable talent for languages (she spoke the Beijing and Shanghai dialects of Chinese, as well as Japanese), she met with many rich and powerful people and government officials from China, who were proud to have friendly relations with this elegant woman."

They would describe her over and over:

"Those breasts, that waist . . ."

At the age of 45 and childless, Xie was famous for her flamboyance, which made some people uneasy.

Especially when she was wearing a silk qipao.

The qipao, once the traditional dress of Manchu women, came to signify the national dress of the Republic of China, though it was not commonly worn by Taiwanese women. It was called the "Shanghai Gown" owing to its popularity and Chinese characteristics.

At its most extreme, the qipao revealed a woman's full body curves, especially when it was a thin, tight-fitting silk garment. It not only accentuated the outline of the wearer's breasts, waist, and buttocks, but, with the high side slits, coquettishly allowed glimpses of the wearer's thighs and calves. As a concession to the conservative nature of Chinese culture, it had a high, nearly airtight neckline collar.

This type of qipao was not commonly worn by Taiwanese. It would become (at least for the next fifty years) the working uniform of bar girls. As with others, they showed off the girls' figures, with the difference that the lining beneath their clinging dresses covered only strategic places. In the winter, they changed into velvet dresses decorated with fake pearls and jade or embroidered with tacky phoenixes.

The same qipaos, but made with finer material, more elegant patterns, and stylish cuts were worn by Madame Chiang Kai-shek, the wife of the man who came from China to rule Taiwan. Her style and elegance became fashionable for a time both in China and abroad. At the time, the wives of ordinary officials all imitated her style.

Wearing qipaos, especially silk ones, was a status symbol.

Later, when more and more women were changing to Western-style clothing, since it was more convenient for work, qipaos fell out of fashion. A popular saying went:

"Only bar girls (or dancing girls) and officials' wives always wear qipaos."

At the time, Xie Xuehong wore silk qipaos, gold necklaces, and diamond rings when she socialized with KMT commanders and county chiefs who had come to rule Taiwan. Her attire was an imitation of the KMT officials' wives. The only difference perhaps was:

Obasan wore silk qipaos.

(However, not long afterwards, Xie would be ostracized by both Taiwan and Chinese governments for having been a bar girl—the kind of woman, apart from officials' wives, who wore qipaos.)

As for Xie's residence above the Da Hua Restaurant, "it was close to the street, a room of about twenty square meters covered with tatami mats. There was a small cupboard and a short writing desk. Hanging on one side of the wall was a haiku scroll given to her by a correctional officer in the Japanese prison, and on the other her special KMT party card."

She would point to the card and say:

"I joined the KMT back when they were cooperating with the Chinese Communist Party, and now I've joined a second time."

Once the leader of the Taiwanese Communist Party, Xie hung Japanese haiku (a gift from her prison correctional officer) and the KMT party card on her walls. When the advance members of the KMT takeover teams came to gather intelligence, she listed the names of guests at the Da Hua Restaurant. There were mayors, county chiefs, some division commanders, regimental commanders, and members of Three Principles of the People Youth Group—all members of the KMT.

Yet she stored large quantities of copper scraps and old copper coins under her tatami in preparation for making ammunition.

Yang Kehuang also worked there. Visitors often saw him seated cross-legged on the tatami, writing at the short desk. The editor of *Peace Daily's* Japanese edition, he was adept at writing short satirical essays. He and Xie were said to be inseparable.

Apart from socializing with people of all types, Xie Xuehong was also regarded as entrepreneurial. She set up a flourishing cold-drinks stand she called Lu Ming Guan in the roadside courtyard of the Da Hua Restaurant, selling shaved ice refreshments in the summer. When KMT officers took possession of airplanes left behind by the Japanese, they sprayed them with salt water to speed up the rusting process, so they could be turned into scrap metal. Xie took the opportunity to buy up the scrap metal and resell it at a significant profit, which was later used to buy arms for resistance troops after the 2/28 Incident.

She won the respect of many people who would not have called her Obasan, the term used in her inner circle; instead, they addressed her respectfully as:

Xie xiansheng, Mr. [Madame] Xie.

They even went so far as to not even say her name, just Xiansheng.

Besides her widely recognized talent at delivering inflammatory speeches, she was also noted for singing a sorrowful Taiwanese folk song:

> Mending the Fishnet
> When I saw the fishnet, my eyes welled up
> Such a gaping hole
> I waited to mend it, yet without any tools
> Who knew my heart ached
> If I did nothing
> There would never be any hope.

This song depicts the hardships of the working class; it also implies a bleak future for the Taiwanese people, making it her favorite song. It was not only popular during the Japanese occupation and after the war, but continued to be sung for another fifty years under a de facto occupation (some even regarded KMT rule as crueler than that of the foreign Japanese), and became testimony to the people's sorrow.

People also believed that Xie Xuehong liked to sing 'The Rainy Night Flower":

> The rainy night flower, the rainy night flower
> Falling from the wind and rain
> No one notices, but it sighs day after day
> The fallen flower on the ground will never return

This song uses flowers to imply women's doomed fate; the following lyrics paint even sadder images: "Heartless rain; heartless rain; plunges me into the pond of suffering; how can you separate me from my leaves and branches; once the petals fall, nothing can be done!" Originally a sorrowful song describing an ordinary woman's helpless fate, it was picked up by prostitutes, who viewed themselves as ruined flowers in the dark night, deprived of sympathy.

As Xie Xuehong was labelled a bar girl by officials from both Taiwan and China, people naturally assumed that she enjoyed singing this song.

My Third Uncle especially loved to talk about the Xie Xuehong of this time. After examining statements by authorities and privately circulating anecdotes, he came to the conclusion that:

"It's true that Xie Xuehong had been a bar girl. However, it was a cover, a means of extracting information from enemies, in the manner of Kawashima Yoshiko, dealing with Japanese, the Chinese Communist Party, and the KMT. Caught between the Chinese and the Taiwanese, it was all she could do."

"She was a bar girl selling her body, but only to serve a real job," Third Uncle emphasized repeatedly.

We therefore thought we knew the Xie Xuehong he described.

My Third Uncle even seriously defended Xie by saying:

"She lived above the Da Hua Restaurant, where she had her own staircase, away from all sorts of people downstairs. When undercover people came by, no one knew whether they were there to dine at the restaurant or to visit her. This provided protection for her underground work, which was the only way she could work in secret. and allowed her to engage in her clandestine work. This is called kabā (Japanese for cover)."

Not until many years later did we learn why Third Uncle defended Xie Xuehong so strongly. It was related to his unwillingness to talk about his own experience in the 2/28 Incident, the island-wide massacre carried out by the Nationalist Government on February 28, 1947, and the ensuing four decades of White Terror. This clearly affected Third Uncle, who loved to talk and to gossip.

2

February 28, 1947, the 2/28 Incident erupted.

People generally believed that the reason for the Incident was, after the war ended and the Japanese had left, the new government from the "motherland," for which people in Taiwan had originally had high expectations, made a complete mess of the takeover. The personnel were corrupt; they monopolized power, positions, and benefits; and the military police acted without law or discipline. This resulted in food shortages and serious inflation. The "motherland" government acted as conquerors who looked down on Taiwanese people as colonial subjects, which led to an accumulation of unresolvable discontent and confrontations.

Auntie Tiger

The powder keg was finally ignited on February 27, 1947. A simple investigation into untaxed cigarettes in front of Taipei's Tianma Tea House resulted in the killing of a bystander. The next day, a crowd gathered in the square in front of the Governor's Office demanding reforms. The military police were ordered to open fire, killing and wounding dozens of people. The "2/28 Incident" quickly engulfed all of Taiwan.

Xie Xuehong won respect for her insightful views on the current state of affairs. More than a year earlier, she had started to deploy resources, so that on the third day after the Incident, the 2nd of March, more than a thousand people from central Taiwan gathered at the Taichung Theater for a citizens' assembly and chose her as chairperson. After the assembly, they began a protest march, confiscated the weapons of the Taichung Monopoly Bureau, and surrounded the house of the county chief and the police station. For a while, the crowd took over all the party, government, and military organizations in central Taiwan.

People who both supported and opposed her, even KMT party members, praised Xie's heroic behavior.

When the crowd brought up gasoline cans to burn down the Taichung county chief's house, she stopped them for fear that the fire might spread to ordinary peoples' houses.

"She jumped off the truck and walked alone toward County Chief Liu and his colleagues. People said it was too dangerous and tried to stop her, but she went ahead anyway, and ordered her people to put down their weapons. When Magistrate Liu recognized Xie Xuehong, he cried out for her help. Xie confiscated the six pistols and sent the offenders to the police station."

An important KMT member who was arrested recalled:

"I saw a truck full of weapons and armed police on the left side of the road driving toward us. At the front of the truck stood a woman carrying a pistol in one hand and waving a white flag with the other. We fired warning shots and ordered it to stop. The woman told the truck driver to do so, and then came alone to talk to us. We recognized her as the famous communist Xie Xuehong, who urged us to put down our weapons and said she would guarantee our safety."

"But when we got onto the truck, the crowd came from all sides to surround us and clamored for us to be handed over to them for punishment. Xie told the crowd that these criminals were prisoners, and under due process would be tried and executed by the authorities. They could not be subjected to mob justice. When she finished talking, the crowd quieted down a little."

"She then ordered the driver to drive off slowly, but not directly to the police station; instead we drove up and down the busy streets. She stopped from time to time to give speeches to the crowd. From what I could tell, she wanted the crowd to know that we had been taken prisoner in order to heighten their rebellious spirit."

Owing to her courage, insight, and resourcefulness, Xie Xuehong emerged as a heroine who led the people of central Taiwan in the 2/28 armed uprising. Even though the local gentry and political leaders organized a "Settlement Committee" to resolve the incident peacefully by means of compromise, Xie continued her armed confrontation strategy.

After confiscating Japanese weapons, Xie appealed to the youth to join the fight. The next day (March 3rd) she formed a Taichung Area Public Order Committee Combat Headquarters, which served as a stronghold for the resistance movement in central Taiwan and welcomed reinforcements from all over.

Within a day, her armed forces assumed control over all the Taichung party, political, military, and military police organizations.

Xie Xuehong and Yang Kehuang originally hoped that Zhang Zhizhong, who had established the "Chiayi Autonomous Allied Force," could come to Taichung to lead the armed forces, which were swiftly expanding with recruits from all over Taiwan. But Zhang needed to remain in Chiayi and was unable to join them. The three of them then decided to select the finest troops to form a core unit they named the 27 Brigade.

However, on March 9, the KMT government brought in military reinforcements from China, the 21st Division. They landed at Keelung and initiated a bloody suppression all over Taiwan. On March 12, the 27 Brigade decided to retreat from Taichung into the mountainous area in Puli, which Xie Xuehong vowed to defend.

Only 2 days later (March 14), Xie and Yang left in a hurry after meeting with someone who called himself Xie Fu, notifying the 27 Brigade's Deputy Commander Zhou Ming (a.k.a Gu Ruiyun): "There is an urgent matter we must attend to, something too involved to explain in a few sentences. You will understand later; do not tell anyone we have left."

Xie would later be denounced in China for this departure and be accused of the criminal charge of:

"2/28 deserter."

My Third Uncle could describe in vivid detail many incidents, including the "Tapani Incident" and "Wushe incident," as if he had been an eyewitness.

That was not the case with the 2/28 Incident, which he actually did experience. For a very long while, not only did he never mention it, he would also sternly caution us whenever we touched upon politics, saying: "Children should be seen and not heard."

As a former neighborhood chief for the Japanese, after the Japanese surrendered and the KMT government began its rule in Taiwan, Third Uncle often made critical comments like the following:

"The Japanese were very strict. If people were caught stealing or some other offense, they would be subjected to water torture or severe beatings; on the other hand, they were disciplined and followed the rules. Unlike the KMT soldiers in rags and straw sandals, with their lecherous, money-grubbing behavior, and indecent acts."

Third Uncle admired the Japanese soldiers' appearance and discipline and looked down on those soldiers who came from China in rags and straw sandals, carrying pans and cups on their backs.

"Those mainlanders frequently said we should thank them for saving us Taiwanese from being conquered people and from receiving Japanese slavery education. They laughed at us for being unable to speak the 'national language' and for wearing geta. What was there to laugh about? The turtle laughing at the tortoise for having no tail."

After the 2/28 Incident, he not only stopped criticizing, but also never again mentioned China's KMT government, especially the army.

But for Third Uncle, even if it meant he could be labelled a "red" and be locked up, he simply could not bear to give up talking about some things. He developed an indirect method to choose certain topics about which he would die if he did not comment.

For a time, he ignored others' viewpoints and insisted that all these years, Xie Xuehong had been hiding somewhere in the central mountain range, with a large stash of weapons left by the Japanese. She'd been waiting for the right time for her comeback:

"It was an impossible operation. No matter how large a stash of weapons she controlled, it was no match for the KMT's national armed forces. Xie was sure to be defeated."

Then he would praise the straw-sandal-wearing KMT soldiers whom he had previously denigrated. He would use the most flattering words he could conjure up to describe them, as if they were troops from heaven. He was also critical of the soldiers, with their cache of weapons, who were hiding out with Xie Xuehong in the central mountain range, where even clouded leopards were rarely seen:

"They have no idea of the danger they face, and they will lose for sure."

Third Uncle did not just emphasize this; he truly believed it. However, it must have given him some comfort to say over and over that Xie

Auntie Tiger

Xuehong hid out in the mountains, waiting for the right time to rise again. It must have helped him face what later happened to him, his relatives, neighbors, friends, and local gentry, who were imprisoned, executed, or went missing for being implicated in the 2/28 Incident.

In order to sustain that last little bit of comfort over something that was clearly not possible, Third Uncle defended other of Xie Xuehong's activities; though he dared not praise her openly, he no longer criticized her.

We'd always been especially frightened by the phrase:

"Here comes Xie Xuehong!"

It replaced such warnings as:

"Here comes Auntie Tiger!"

"Here comes a wolf!"

"Here come the police!"

For a long time, it was an effective means of making children behave, so long as the adults said it with a somewhat fearful look and in a low voice:

"Here comes Xie Xuehong."

Even the naughtiest kids would stop making noise, stop crying, pretend to be asleep (in the end, as the adults wished, they'd fall asleep), or finish their homework and do as they were told.

Why were we so afraid of "Here comes Xie Xuehong!"? Until then, what scared us most were the phrases: "Here comes Auntie Tiger!" and "Here come the police!"

We had seen the police and knew what they were capable of: they could handcuff us, they could take us away from home, our parents, and our playmates, and they could even shoot us dead.

As to Auntie Tiger, we had never seen her, but children all knew that she was a tiger who had transformed herself into an aunt. One day she went to A-Jin and A-Yin's home. No matter how hard she tried, she could not hide her tail, and instead of the chair A-Jin moved over for her, she had to sit on an urn. (We had to watch out for people who came to visit us; if anyone asked for an urn to sit on, we would know this person was Auntie Tiger, who needed to hide her tail.)

We could never sleep with strangers at night for fear it might be Auntie Tiger, who gobbled up foolish A-Jin; A-Yin did not realize that Auntie Tiger was eating A-Jin's fingers until he asked what she was eating. Auntie Tiger replied:

"Raw ginger! So crispy; have one."

She tossed over a bloody finger.

(We avoided eating crispy things; the "ka-cha" sound of chewing was like eating a finger, which stopped us from chewing, and we would quickly swallow whatever we had in our mouth. Also, if we saw someone eating in bed under a mosquito net, we would follow A-Yin's example by saying we needed to pee. Auntie Tiger would tie a rope around us, and, like A-Yin, tie the other end to the chamber pot, so when she pulled the rope, she'd feel the weight and know we were still there. But we only had a toilet in the house, no chamber pot.)

Anyhow, we had to run away quickly, but no matter how far we ran, Auntie Tiger would catch us. We knew tigers can run fast, but cannot climb high, so we'd be safe by climbing a tree.

(What if we couldn't find a tree, since there weren't many near us?)

Even if we managed to climb up a tree, she could still bite through the tree trunk with her sharp teeth. So we had to lie: "I'll jump off the tree for you to eat me; I can't run away, anyway."

To make us tastier, we suggested she heat up a pot of oil in the kitchen and hang it over a branch, and then wait below with her mouth open, while we fried ourselves in the oil before jumping straight into her mouth. (Of course, we'd pour the hot oil over her. But we weren't very good at tree climbing and chances were we might fall out of the tree. Or we'd fail to trick her. Or maybe we didn't have any oil at home. Or we couldn't climb a tree in the first place.)

That's why we were so scared of "Here comes Auntie Tiger!" Even though we knew she was a tiger in disguise, we memorized ways to identify her, to be vigilant so we could run away. Whether any of the means worked or not, at least we were well prepared.

Nonetheless, we knew nothing about "Xie Xuehong." Grownups would not say anything about her. They just looked so frightened, which meant she must be even scarier than Auntie Tiger. Worse yet, they'd never taught us how to deal with her when she came. (They wouldn't even allow us to mention her name.)

That frightened us even more.

For a long time, if we had been frightened to tears by the line "Here comes Xie Xuehong!" adults would follow up with: "Stop crying, or Xie Xuehong will really come." That would scare us so badly we'd immediately shut up.

We always remembered the fear that we could not express with our tears.

"Here comes Xie Xuehong!"

Even though Third Uncle had praised the KMT soldiers as if they'd been sent from heaven and changed his tone in insisting that an exhausted Xie Xuehong had been stuck in the high Central Mountain range, where even clouded leopards were seldom seen, that did not spare him from calamity. After the 2/28 Incident's "appeasement" massacre had engulfed the whole island, an era of White Terror began, during which he was implicated and imprisoned.

Lacking any evidence of a crime, he was guilty only of "commenting on current events." Our family spent a large sum of money to get him out of prison. Though he did not stay there long, my talkative Third Uncle never mentioned his prison experience. Given the times, everyone in our family kept quiet, as if it had never happened.

Third Uncle and our family weren't the only silenced ones; everyone in Lukang was silent. Later, people stopped talking about anything related not only to the Incident but also to "politics."

But to the government, "politics" could include almost anything having to do with government, public affairs, even discussions of current events.

Nonetheless, the "Incident we could not mention, let alone related documents, writings, and images, existed in a form so vague and so enormous that it became a ubiquitous reality that shackled us for a very long time.

We knew for sure it existed.

(We just knew.)

There were beggars and lunatics everywhere. Perhaps not many actually witnessed the massacre during the Incident, but many did see dead bodies openly laid out at train stations, in front of radio stations, at city halls, in parks, and on riverbanks. Even though the bodies were taken away or pushed into the river or pits at night, murmurs about the incident started to spread after the bloodstains had dried. They snowballed as people privately passed on stories. In the following decades, stories that featured body parts, human hair, scooped out hearts, lungs, intestines, and stomachs flowing out of opened bellies, eyeballs, and decomposing bones, were spread by people who did not have family or friends involved in the Incident, that is, those who had less to fear.

But those who did have relatives, friends, or neighbors who had gone missing, had been killed, or were locked up in prison pretended that nothing had happened and would keep quiet even when asked.

People spoke of an unburied coffin or two in a derelict house that was about to collapse. When night fell, the crazy offspring of the deceased sat or squatted on the coffins, laughing shrilly or howling all night long. Yet, as dawn broke, they vanished with the dark night without a trace, as if they had never existed.

Then there were people who wandered the streets day and night, muttering to themselves, sometimes raising their voices as if cursing. When people approached them, they froze in alarm. Afraid to make a sound, the sudden silence seemed to take their breath away.

There were also people who stood at the same spot every day, rain or shine, without saying a word, waiting and watching, eyes fixed straight ahead. They were like specters planted among people who kept moving forward. They held on to a point when time froze, and as everything stopped for them, the crowd in motion could even walk through their bodies.

There were a good many mad people whose family or neighbors supplied them with food; otherwise, they could not have survived. Nonetheless, no one came forward for them, and they simply lived on with nothing, while we existed in an unreal world.

And there were beggars everywhere, including an old woman with her grandchild coming out of nowhere, humiliated to be asking for money. She did not behave like ordinary beggars, more like a passerby in need of travelling money for the next, unknown stop.

They appeared suddenly, stayed briefly, and were never seen again.

There were sick old people stuck in places, too. There was an old woman whom people in the neighborhood got to know as Meihua. For months she had sneaked into a small Earth God Temple during the night with her four grandsons. She was crippled with an infected, swollen, and festering leg. For fear that she would be driven out of the temple during the day, she crawled out and stayed under a nearby banyan tree, while her grandsons, with malignant boils and fungus-covered scalps, went out begging.

Then one day, Meihua and her four grandsons, who seemed to have materialized, left without a trace.

A vague, hushed rumor had it that the military police had taken them away on a truck. Meihua was actually an undercover communist spy; her crippled leg was the result of a sophisticated makeup job, and the four children had been kidnapped to give her convenient cover.

As to why Meihua was an enemy spy, that too had its source in the "Incident" . . .

It was an era of mad people and beggars. We did not witness the massacre, we did not see piled bodies or bloodstains, and even Third Uncle seldom passed on his tales. Our fear came from having been taught that one could not believe even what one witnessed, for there had to be a conspiracy by enemy spies.

Having said that, could it be that what we feared the most—"Here comes Xie Xuehong!"—was a hoax? If so, would that mean that Xie Xuehong would not come? But what if "Xie Xuehong would not come!" was the conspiracy, then that really meant we had fallen into the trap!

Here comes Xie Xuehong.

The Xie Xuehong who came was elaborately described this way:

She had long, wavy black hair, parted on the side. One side was tucked behind her ear with a diamond hair pin, the other side hung down, nearly covering one eye, her eyebrow, and half of her cheek. She had a languid look, drowsy and coquettish, as if she'd just climbed out of bed after sex.

She had heavy eyebrows and high cheek bones; thick, sexy red lips; and a haughty look; her blood-red lips were parted, as if always waiting to be kissed.

Of course, she would wear silk qipaos (we kept seeing in magazines and newspapers that the wife of the ruler from China, Madame Chiang Kai-shek, and other officials' wives wore silk qipaos). We could not understand why those qipaos had such high, tight collars that covered the wearers' necks, which we thought could be exposed with no harm. Yet they had high splits up both sides, so that the wearers' legs were in full view as they walked. Luckily, they also wore black fishnet stockings and garters embroidered with black roses.

As for women's breasts, which we thought should never be exposed, qipaos pushed them up high with their tight-fitting style. The sheer, body-hugging silk qipaos outlined the wearers' every curve.

She held a long, obligatory pipe in her hand, and for that she wore a cut-in sleeveless gown that showed off her jade-white arms (she sometimes wore elbow-length gloves). She held the thin, nearly foot-long pipe between her diamond-ringed index and middle fingers. She would inhale and then blow the smoke out, her squinty eyes misty, with a wanton gaze.

There were no photos of Xie Xuehong. People were afraid to be identified and implicated in the 2/28 Incident, so they destroyed or hid all such photos to protect themselves. That is why the "bar girl" image of Xie Xuehong was instilled in our minds.

What frightened us most was the furtive rumor that if you took away the silk qipaos, long gloves, pipe, and stockings worn by the "bar girl" Xie Xuehong, you would find something different down there.

What "down there"? What was different? How was it different? We learned nothing, and when we pressed for clarification, all we got were ambiguous replies like "It's just different." Or "that was different" . . .

A furtive rumor spread that a "bad woman" like her did not wear underpants. That is to say, those high split silk qipaos were so easily lifted up (without taking them off), that an effortless hoisting (the thin silky fabric was no obstacle), revealed a vagina forever waiting between open legs (for any man to penetrate).

The "down there" was dense with intrigues.

We also learned that it was not possible to wear underpants under qipaos that exposed legs up to the buttocks.

(Does that mean there was nothing under the qipaos worn by the model for all nation's women, Madame Chiang Kai-shek, and those officials' wives?)

Underpants became a symbol of safety to us, from which we understood the meaning of lasciviousness, all having to do with wearing underpants, taking them off, or not wearing them at all.

In the eyes of the Chinese who came to rule Taiwan over the following five decades, Xie's legacy from the 2/28 Incident in the homeland she fled was that of:

A bar girl.

Many years after the Incident, people were still saying that she had hidden out in the high Central mountains, accessible only to clouded leopards. In fact, she had not led troops and taken large quantities of weapons left behind by the Japanese into the mountains, as rumored.

On the contrary, on March 14, Xie and Yang Kehuang secretively left the 27 Brigade base. In China, where she would live during various political struggles for more than twenty years, this clandestine departure proved her guilt as:

A 2/28 deserter.

She later explained to the then leader of the 27 Brigade, Zhou Ming:

"On the night of March 14, Xie Fu came with an communique from the provincial working committee that the situation had become extremely perilous and that party members must cease all open resistance and go into hiding in order to protect the strength of the organization."

In that chaotic situation, party leadership and discipline were neither clear nor strict; people generally believed that Xie used that as an acceptable excuse to leave, and not unnecessarily sacrifice herself as a "martyr," so she could make a comeback in the future. Her decision and belief were likely based on what she had learned and fought through all those years, from an impoverished background and from being a child bride and a concubine.

However, she would surely be condemned as a leader who neither fought to the end with her comrades nor arranged to break up the 27 Brigade so they could find a way out and join up with other guerrillas.

Before leaving, she left Zhou Ming with a means of contacting her:

"Go to the town of Zhushan and ask for Zhang Zaotian. He died during the attack on Chiayi Airport, and his mother is the only one left in the family. Put your hands together to pay your respects and ask her for three incense sticks; then bow three times to his memorial tablet. That way she'll know you are one of us and will bring you to me."

Zhou Ming had withdrawn to Puli with slightly more than two hundred men, a unit hastily formed with civilians. On March 15, after a brief battle with KMT troops from the 21st Division at Wuniunan, they dispersed and fled.

Zhou Ming followed Xie Xuehong's instruction to join her at Zhushan; they then set out for Xiaomei, where Chen Zuandi was based. But Xie had second thoughts, as she did not know Chen well; she had heard only that he had joined Malayan guerrillas. So, they decided not to go to Xiaomei.

On March 25, Xiaomei fell to the KMT, who reportedly began searching door to door for them. The three of them fled Zhushan that night.

Yang Kehuang suggested they go to hide at his brother-in-law's in Zhanghua City. They walked in the mountains for seven or eight hours in the dark, arriving in Zhanghua at dawn. As Yang's brother-in-law was looking after them, he passed on what he had heard on the streets: The 27 Brigade had thousands of men, who had killed hundreds of KMT soldiers. They needed dozens of trucks just to carry away the bodies. The brigade had then withdrawn to Wushe along with a number of Japanese soldiers.

The three of them listened and laughed but said nothing.

Later the news broke that: "Xie Xuehong has sneaked into Zhanghua, and a police search is underway."

They decided to split up. It would be too conspicuous for Xie and Yang to travel together, so Xie went with Zhou Ming, who was only 22 years old, to Dadu Township. Yang went to hide at his brother's house in Fengshan in southern Taiwan.

Xie Xuehong dressed as a country woman, wearing an old cotton top and pants, covering her face with a straw hat. The only giveaway were her un-peasantlike clean hands. She had to hide them under her shirt; but the weather in central Taiwan in late March was hot and the rice seedlings had grown tall, and no one would put their hands under their clothes to keep warm.

Luckily, Zhou Ming stood in front of her as cover, so they did not draw the attention of the military police patrolling the train.

That train, to us, was always a death trap.

(Third Uncle's involvement in the 2/28 Incident allegedly also occurred on a train.)

Trains became killing zones, taking more lives than city halls, radio stations, army barracks, parks, even the plazas in front of train stations. The reason was simple: moving trains that carried our earnest hope to escape would in the end trap us without providing any exit.

When a moving train was controlled by military police who were searching for and arresting suspicious people, the only way to halt a journey with a set destination and unvarying track was to jump while the train was moving, virtually assuring our death.

Even if we successfully jumped off the train before the enemy identified us, we still would have been terrified, waiting for armed police as they searched for suspicious characters and fugitives, one railcar after another.

The "suspicious characters" could be anyone who looked literate because they had the ability to think.

Those who needed to be eliminated were not limited to those few escaping defeated rebels or saboteurs; they really wanted to uproot and eliminate "intellectuals," those who looked literate, for they were the reactionary cause of all disasters.

For that reason alone, on the moving train it could be fatal for anyone who had slender, fair hands that had not been exposed to the sun, were soft to touch, and had no bulging knuckles from hard labor.

If that were not enough, a pair of white, delicate feet that had seldom gone without shoes was sufficient reason to be arrested or shot on the spot.

(Third Uncle had hardly ever done any heavy labor. It was said a kind-hearted farmer had hidden him under his seat and shielded him by placing a sack of peanuts between his legs. This move saved my literate Third Uncle from revealing his delicate white hands, which could have got him killed.)

The moving high-speed train seemed to be fleeing to safety; however, it could only run on the set tracks and must have presented another kind of predicament, which was taking us toward an unknown and likely fatal ending.

In her nightmare, there was always a moving train.

She must have been in Russia, as there were long narrow sleeping berths. She had to be dreaming, for how else could she explain the sugarcane fields flying past the train windows? The ripening sugarcane was taller than a man. Their long, thick purple stalks poked out from withered leaves. Standing over the hills and plains were these weird purple objects with hard bulging nodes like weapons of war waiting to be used.

It must have been a dream, for how could there be sugarcane fields in Russia? There were even people hawking lunch boxes made of thin strips of wood. When you opened them, there was sour black bread.

(If only it had been white rice. Shredded sweet potatoes with rice would do.)

It must have been a dream; otherwise why was the train carrying sugarcane in its sleeping berths? Bundles of purple stalks were like limbs oozing congealed blood that filled every sleeping berth.

(Were purple sugarcane stalks sleeping in all the berths?)

The train turned into a narrow gauge "sugar train"? That was a relief, as she was no longer on a Russian train running in Taiwanese sugarcane fields. Wasn't this the Imperial Sugar Factory's narrow-gauge train used to transport sugarcane? There were bundles of sugarcane still with their withered dry leaves, long and rigid, still sharp and prickly. All of a sudden, she had a sickle in her hand. She had been hired to scrape off the dried leaves, so the sugarcane stalks could be sent to the mill to have the sweet juice pressed out to make sugar. She gave it a try with the sickle, but what emerged from the wrapped leaves was not sugarcane, but purple corpses with congealed blood.

Try another sugarcane bundle! She was, after all, hired to scrape off the leaves. Several slices of the sickle still revealed corpses.

Was it her permanent job to cut out bodies from withered leaves with a sickle? In the end, each slice of the sickle produced corpses from bundles of leafy sugarcane.

(How many bundled corpses could this long train carry? Like leafless maroon sugarcane stalks thirty, even fifty to a bundle. How many purple corpses with congealed blood could a rail car hold?)

A long train with at least a dozen rail cars stuffed with bundles of dead people, how many could there be?

Or how many bundles of sugarcane?

She woke up and, for a moment, did not know where she was. She couldn't think straight. Was this Moscow? Japan? Or Shanghai?

A sudden panic attack made her sit up. Her bamboo bed creaked, a familiar sound caused merely by simply turning over.

She was still on the run, still in Taiwan.

She was on her guard, ready to flee at a moment's notice. Then she sensed a man sleeping beside her. (Different men had accompanied her during her prolonged flight. Who could this be?). At least she wasn't worried, so she remained motionless to listen carefully. There were only the endless sounds of croaking frogs and chirping insects out in the fields.

In the dark, she gradually recognized simple objects that were what she'd thought they were. She looked carefully to chase away the fear that made her gasp for air. In the corner of the room was a shabby old chest of drawers whose second drawer held the blue Taiwanese shirt and pants she had with her at all times. She was not sure if the low wooden table and stools for meals were in the center of the room. As expected, the smaller objects came into view as if they were squatting or lying on the floor.

Seized by an intense desire to be hugged, she shut her eyes and wrapped her arms around her chest so tightly she was out of breath; her face turned hot and red. By contrast, her lower body seemed empty and open. After relaxing her arms, she sat up, wrapped her arms around her knees and curled up.

The bamboo bed creaked with her every movement; outside, the frogs still croaked and the insects chirped noisily, the sounds thudding against her chest. There was a chill in the countryside on that April night, and she felt immensely lonely.

(Tung oil flowers were in full bloom in the mountain forests of central Taiwan, snowy white clusters on the tips of the new branches, like clouds sitting atop green twigs. It felt so familiar I must have been here in a previous life.)

I glimpsed the fleeting scenery out of the corner of my eye and must have seen the man beside me at that moment, picturing him through the gaps of lush tung oil branches, leaves, and clusters of cloud-like flowers.

Why was I always dreaming of intimacy on the cloud-like, fragrant flower bed, my naked body slowly spreading out like a flower waiting for your body to press down on mine and enter into my flower heart under layers of petals that would then fall and curl up after being rubbed and kneaded?

Had our bodies already intertwined among the cloud-like white petals, leaving me with an eternal desire for the most affectionate love?

In this vast deserted wasteland, what I ached for was the intertwining of our bodies, surrounded by petals, which I thought might be the last sexual intercourse of my life.

Therefore, intertwine, climb high, fuse, rest.

It was the last place to which I could return.

Ah! Why was it necessary to force the toxic xionghuang liquor down my throat? Such a hopeless situation, such a bleak wasteland makes someone as helpless and self-protective as me want to gradually cast off every bit of my old self as a woman and return to my most primitive basic instinct.

With that mindset I made love as if it might be the last time, but also as if I was reenacting the first time. Surrounded by fragrant petals, among leaves and branches, I stretched out a new woman's body.

My last time and my very first time.

And I knew, it was, without doubt, your first time.

In this desperate, turbulent time, I needed to hide myself in your warmth, a reliable place where I could ensure that my new woman's body would not be frightened back to my original state with nothing to hold onto all of a sudden.

After experiencing these ordeals, I began to have a sense of this strange woman's body I'd turned into, and I asked you to—

Make me become a woman one last time!

(While I still could.)

The man said he'd slept lightly on the floor beside the bamboo bed. He was alarmed to be woken up, until he heard the woman say softly.

"Come to bed."

Still sleepy, he obeyed, as usual.

She reached out and held him.

The man said he thought foreigners were all like this. She'd behaved this way because of her Soviet experience. When she kissed him, kissed him hard on the lips, he said he thought this was a foreign custom.

His unresponsiveness made her sob.

"I've sacrificed my life for revolution, sacrificed my youth. Now with my youth gone, my life could end at any time."

The man said she said: "It must be fate that we're together like this."

When she reached down and held him, he knew what it meant to be serious.

The man said she was crying when she said: "Take pity on me, comfort me..."

She continued to fondle, touch, softly rub and tickle.

"This is a great comfort to me, body and soul..."

The man said he gave in and accepted what she said.

(I touched your virginal body and knew I must possess this youthful, glorious body, to ensure that you would not betray me.)

My cold, dangerous, slippery body wrapped around your burning hot frame, which radiated heat after being aroused and guided by me. I covered you entirely.

I absorbed your body heat first.

I needed the heat to help me unfold; with enough warmth, I would stretch and spread out long so you could come inside me.

My ice-cold hand glided over your chest, where it lingered. Here was my eternal memory; I would know, without the slightest reminder, for thousands of ages, that in the piping hot blood, a vigorously beating heart full of emotions and the smells of heat and blood were what I'd longed for all my life.

However, at that moment my womanly hands would avoid this heart, for the heat of that heart, under his chest and beneath my smooth hands, was not sufficient for me and not what I needed at the moment.

What I wanted was another way of "heart to heart."

And so, I took you inside me. Your cock, which had never experienced the acts of penetrating and thrusting, would learn to remember this first time. I deepened and engraved my exclusive mark on your cock as you continue to thrust in and out from now on. You will come back to me for more. You will seek the familiar match of length and shape in order to feel reassured.

I also made sure to give you the utmost pleasure, which you could not easily obtain anywhere else. Even if you occasionally wandered off, you would still come back time and time again.

Holding your cock meant I had a grip on your heart.

So, I was not afraid you would betray me. Not only did I have the first memory of your cock, I was also sure that if I could repeatedly match its most deeply held memory, I could have you again and again.

There was no way you would betray me, for you needed to keep returning to me.

For me, the cock that entered a woman's body for the very first time also took me back to the sensation of the first time I was penetrated. This inexperienced little thing surrendered inside me in a very short time, leaving me unaroused and unsatisfied.

As it turned out, I seriously felt the unfamiliarity of the inside of my body. It was as if in the woman's body I was slowly losing there were still unknown chambers waiting to be developed. Only after I had been penetrated, aroused, and satisfied did I know that a place exists in a woman's body that can generate sexual pleasure.

I had to be used in order to know I still had a woman's body, not that of a fox or a raccoon or a snake or a fish.

Nonetheless, you were incapable of using me to make me feel the sensuality of a woman's body; conversely, I wrapped you up tightly to engrave on your cock its first memory of a woman's body. Subsequently, this would also serve as a reconfirmation of becoming a woman for the first time.

In a way, by creating a new woman's body for you, I owned you with that body, so that you would not betray me.

At least for now, temporarily, that was all I needed.

She did not, as rumor had it, hide out in the central mountain range where clouded leopards were seldom seen.

They were searching for a new way out, and Yang Kehuang was far away in southern Taiwan at a fishing harbor looking for a fishing boat willing to smuggle them out of Taiwan. The less noticeable Zhou Ming had three days to make contact.

She verified his activities during those three days, even sending someone to his house to check. He thought:

"No doubt she meant to comfort my family, but on the other hand, it was likely done out of political vigilance, something unique to communists. During complex political struggles, some weak-minded people tend to betray their comrades after being arrested and threatened, intimidated, or bribed."

She once asked him:

"Why do you stay with me? You're a wanted man yourself. Isn't it more dangerous for you to be with an even bigger target, like me?"

He replied:

"It's to protect you, of course. You're a leader of the masses, of the revolution. People need you to live on."

At that time, wanted posters of Xie Xuehong and Yang Kehuang were in all the train stations, with a reward of 200,000 for their arrest.

She said to him in jest:

"Why don't you snitch on me for the reward?"

He replied:

"Sounds good! If your head is worth 200,000, mine is cheaper, but still should be worth no less than 100,000! Let me get the 200,000 for yours and you get the 100,000 for mine. Wouldn't it be great to get rich together!"

5

Nocturnal Strings

Lee Yu
(translated by Chris Wen-chao Li)

Once there was a mist. The lid of the vat is covered in dew. A garden slug traces a sinuous trail. Palm-like papaya leaves cast their shadows onto an upturned face.

The larynx bobbles in sync with the gargling of water.

The foam on the edge of his mouth is wiped away with a towel. The gates creak open behind him.

Enter a woman with elegant features. A northerner, whose broad, pale face shows not a hint of a tan, even in the heat of August. Fair skin aside, though, little remains of her northern roots.

Dressed in a floral-patterned cream coat and long blue trousers, holding a planter full of pinks, she frees a hand to secure the latch behind her, then bends over and utters "Good morning."

"Morning." He smiles and wipes away the water on his cheeks. Peering in through the chapel window, he can see on the wall clock it's early yet—no rush to change clothes.

He gathers his toiletries from the lid of the vat and drapes the towel over his arm, carefully making his way down the steps, toes snug in his wooden clogs.

She retrieves broom, dustpan, brush, and washcloth from the bamboo shed. Water is fetched from the same vat. After sprinkling the evergreens and the pomegranate bush along the wall, she then sets up next to the cobblestone path leading to the front door.

He pushes aside his books, searching every drawer and checking beneath the sheets and pillows, until the black-rimmed glasses he has been looking for over the past two days appears before his eyes. He picks up the newspaper lying on the side table.

Over here, she enters the house, pail in hand. Clear droplets cling to the surface between her fingers as she dips her hands into the cool water and shakes them dry. Little drops of water fall to the ground.

He moves his wooden stool over to the shade beneath the papaya tree, and after adjusting his glasses, opens the newspaper, spreading it across his lap.

With one hand on the side of the bed, she bends over and removes a pair of black oxfords and a pair of black galoshes from under the bed, after which she extends her broom to the farthest edge.

His ginger locks dance in the morning light, filtered through the leaves of the papaya tree. From Ireland he hails, a northern abode of sorts.

She picks up the pillow and gives it a good shake—from whose morning glory pattern drops a tuft of red hair.

The papaya tree bedazzles with flowers in full bloom but does not bear fruit. The English-language newspaper, airmailed from overseas, is printed on paper so thin the words bleed through. It's hard to read. He moves the paper closer. What a pungent odor of ink. The newsprint is already a good eleven or twelve days old, yet it still smudges his fingers.

As usual, he must wash his hands and dry even the lines in his palms on the sides of his robe before he is ready to leaf through the pages of the gilded book.

> *They shall feed in the ways, and their pastures shall be in all high places.*
>
> *They shall not hunger nor thirst; neither shall the heat nor sun smite them: for he that hath mercy on them shall lead them, even by the springs of water shall he guide them.*

The pages, yellowed at the edges, give off the smell of aged wood. Only after gently closing the book was he able to cast off the grit and grime of the past six days and a half and begin to feel, little by little, sufficiently rejuvenated.

Another glance at the clock, and this time, he puts his glasses back into his pocket, folds the newspaper back on its creases, and stands up from his round stool.

Vacating the bedroom and moving to the chapel, she opens a row of wood-frame windows from the bottom. Wind rushes through, stirring up dust on the sacred figurines.

She removes the stale bouquet from the altar vase and places newly cut flowers in it. Fresh water is added to the stoup at the entrance.

By the time she is seated at the organ on the chancel, the sun is shining through the plastic panels of the awning, bathing the fallboard in a soft green hue.

With a fresh washcloth she wipes the fallboard, sending particles of dust flying into the air. She mops the surface repeatedly until the contours of her face appear in the glossy black finish.

Not bad-looking for a woman in her forties—not a wrinkle in sight, judging from her likeness in the black varnish.

She opens the lid and, with fabric wrapped around her index finger, begins to wipe off each black and white key.

Back on her feet, she dusts the carved wooden screen behind the organ, reaching into every crevice to remove the buildup. The wood is restored to its natural brown, the shine and finish of which is rendered visible only once a week.

Behind the screen, occupying an entire corner of the room, is a sizable object veiled under a dark green cover.

"It is off limits," she was told the day she started work here. "Leave it alone. Don't touch it or try to clean it."

She did as told, keeping her distance, treating it as sacred, along with the crucifix, the figurines, the chalice, and the prayer candles.

Wearing a black tunic over his embroidered white cassock, he flings open the doors of the chapel and, gilded bible under his arm, welcomes the first parishioner into his church.

She returns her cleaning supplies to the shed, pats the dust off her chest, pulls her hair together and tucks the loose bits behind her ear, then seeks shelter behind the largest papaya tree.

The soft rays of the morning sun now beam down from overhead. The priest raises his hand and makes the sign of the cross over his impeccably white embroidered cassock.

As he traces a cross over his white polyester garment, row upon row of worshippers genuflect on kneelers, revealing a sea of dark tresses.

> *Our Father who art in heaven,*
> *Hallowed be thy name.*
> *Thy kingdom come,*
> *Thy will be done on earth, as it is in heaven.*

The wind enters yet again through the wood-frame windows, ruffling the pages of a book of morning prayers.

The window frames are green, as are the walls. Sunlight, now much brighter than before, beams through the plastic awning. As the priest turns and raises his chalice, he is surrounded by a haze of green.

Ginger-red hair. Irish pastures. The embroidered white tablecloth flutters in a corner. The leaves of the papaya tree tickle her face.

Incense is lit in the thurible. Smoke envelopes the altar and obscures the congregation in the nave.

She picks up the scent of sandalwood as prayers drift in her direction. The voice of a young woman rises above the din.

The congregation rises, this time to exit the pews in an orderly manner. Worshippers kneel and cross themselves in the aisle, then dip their fingers in the holy water to touch their foreheads. Offerings are dropped into the collection box. The organist plays hymns as the worshippers exit the chapel.

The priest shuts the door and invites her to join in next time, even if it means sitting in a corner in the rear of the chapel.

He lays a missal into her hand as she considers the priest's offer.

A lit candle adorns the cover of the pale blue booklet, which fits snug into her palm.

"We meet at five on Saturdays for an hour."

"Not sure I can find the time—" she says apologetically.

"Then come after mass on Sunday," he urges.

Sundays aren't busy days, she thinks to herself—it probably wouldn't hurt to open up shop a bit later. But lingering trepidation remains.

Passing the market, she buys a pair of knee-length socks from a street vendor to give her a bit of courage.

The priest instructs her to move her chair a little closer and form a circle with the other participants. Under the encouraging gaze of veteran members left and right, she does as told, all the while keeping her head down. Her feet, she notices, are now in the center of an assortment of stylishly chic sandals.

There are five people in the group, all young women from a nearby college, one of whom is always late, showing up red in the face. The priest reminds them that all are equal in the eyes of God, speaking in a voice that is calm and unrushed. She draws her feet back under her seat and does her best to focus, reading softly and answering timidly when it is her turn.

Explaining that she needs ample time to open up the shop or risk upsetting her boss, she makes an excuse to leave.

She slides the missal into her breast pocket and shuts the gate behind her. With the lazy afternoon sun baking the alley, temperatures start to rise.

She undoes the top button of her blouse, then lifts the pot with both arms. Warm water is mixed in with the flour. With business slow on Sunday afternoons, the boss is content to leave the diner to her and spend his time in the attic playing mahjong with his wife.

With both hands on the large wooden mixing spoon, she stirs with all her might, occasionally flattening scraps along the side to test their consistency. With each movement the corner of the missal in her breast pocket pokes against her ribs. Faith brings comfort to our lives, the priest says. The more she stirs, the greater the resistance. Beads of sweat roll down her forehead.

She covers the dough with a moist cloth and picks up the tub and the vegetables.

It isn't long before the water she washed her vegetables in and later dumped onto the roadside is absorbed by the gravel surface. Leaning on the door frame, fingers still wet, she tucks her hair behind her ears and stretches to soothe her mildly sore back.

On Headwater [Suiyuan] Road in the month of September, a chill is in the air, flowing from the end of the street.

A lonely side street, with no pedestrians. The sun's rays slowly draw close to the opening of the lane. With asphalt newly paved, gone are the ruts in the dirt. No longer will she have to put up with stumbling along or kicking up pebbles.

She steps inside and places the vegetable tub on a kitchen shelf, then bends over to prepare the stove.

Before long, the water is brought to a boil. She turns down the heat and allows the liquid to simmer while wiping away the sweat on her brow with the back of her wrist.

The smell of beef, peppercorn, and star anise soon fills the tiny space.

A few square tables and a smattering of wooden stools. Using a wrung-out rag, she wipes each surface once again, so that the regulars will not have to go home with greasy elbows.

These include a few young men living in the dorms, a middle-aged professor who brings his young daughter along to order takeout, and a young working couple.

She gives the meat in the stock pot another stir—the professor likes his shank slices well-cooked.

Well-mannered diners, they always say "please."

"How about some dumplings, sir?" she asks softly. "Or a side of shredded bean curd, sir?"

Chopped green onions are sprinkled over the noodles, which are then doused with a ladle of broth. She wipes away the spillage and serves the dish with a smile.

If only she were better educated, she says to herself.

Sunlight slowly reaches the door, casting elongated shafts of light through the rectangular entrance that bounce off wisps of vapor, bounce off the fuzz on the shoulders of a student's sweater, and bounce off the steam rising from the bowl of noodles in front of him. He removes his glasses and places them on the table, then blows on the piping-hot noodles before slurping them. Sunlight dances on the fine hairs on one side of his face. He turns a page of his book. The sound of shuffling mahjong tiles echoes from upstairs.

She pours herself a glass of water. The light now shines at an angle and is about to disappear behind the legs of the far-side table. A passing commuter bus sends whirls of dust billowing into the air, suspended momentarily in the dying light before settling onto the darkening road surface.

Temperatures drop. She lifts her cup and takes a sip of water, then stands and switches on the ceiling light. Night descends without the slightest warning.

She passes ten windows and fourteen suffering icons as she makes her way through the green aisle of the central nave, her gaze settling eventually on the space behind the papaya trees. The priest has decided to hold a special religious education class in the evening.

She is the only one to show up. After closing up, she braved the still sticky asphalt and walked past two rows of newly installed neon lamps, a bus stop with no one waiting, and a portrait studio displaying photos of smiling co-eds in the window, and from there continued up the slope to Wenzhou Street.

Walking down a dark alley, she heard the clacking of mahjong tiles from beyond the walls, in rhythm with her every footfall on the gravel.

She made a turn, and at the end of two rows of houses a faint light flickered through the slits of a bamboo fence. As she quickened her pace, the plastic soles of her shoe squeaked like chirping insects.

Under a glowing lamp, she turns to page twenty:

> *Don't lose sight of your ultimate end,*
> *Don't cease to nurture the life divine;*
> *Don't turn your back on who you are,*
> *Don't try to hide your past transgressions.*

With light projecting mid-angle, he slowly loses track of his own speech as he lowers his red lashes. Never before has she sat so close to him, close enough to make out the wires supporting his dentures.

The petals on two short-stemmed pinks in a water glass cast shadows on his moving fingers. The faint scent of mothballs or aged wood seems to waft from the sleeves of his dark cassock.

The priest ends his reading and inserts a pencil to mark the page, then removes his glasses and raises his eyelids to reveal irises of a clear chestnut color.

"Wait a second." He smiles at her as he rises from his seat.

The room is quiet but for the ticking of the clock.

In the yellowing light, the pinks turn a flushed red. She straightens up at the table and resigns herself to the relentless barrage of colors coming at her from all directions. Sweet pea shoots climb out of the white pillow sham, their tendrils creeping up to and then off the mattress, and from there to the tabletop. She retracts all ten fingers from the sides of the table and balls up her fists.

The aroma grows ever stronger. She moves her chair forward and presses her chest against the table.

The priest appears at the entrance, smiling.

"Come," he says, opening the door to the kitchen wider and ushering her through.

On the square dining table are two porcelain cups, each already filled with a dark liquid.

The priest motions for her to sit. He uncorks a small bottle, gives it a good whiff, and then adds a few drops to each cup, instantly filling the room with the bouquet of alcohol.

From the minifridge in the corner, he retrieves an open can. He picks up a spoon and flips it over. Slowly, he pours the contents of the can along the backside of the spoon.

A layer of cream now floats atop the dark liquid.

He gently pushes cup and saucer toward her.

She is hesitant, but under his eager, encouraging smile, she brings the cup to her lips, and it dawns on her where that exotic smell had come from.

With the index and middle fingers of both hands, he lifts the red checkered cover in the middle of the table. What comes into view are dinner rolls dusted with flour.

She makes an effort to remember the reason to believe. As she is mincing pork, passages memorized from the lesson prior run through her head.

"You're ready to be baptized," the priest announces reassuringly. "Let's aim for Christmas," he says, cutting a slice of the raisin loaf.

She, on the other hand, is in no hurry, for baptism would mean an end to these meetings.

By now she has learned to slice bread evenly with a serrated knife, add the right consistency of cream so that it stays afloat, and sip the hot liquor-infused coffee beneath layers of cold cream—for once she understands what it is like to have stability in life.

Nocturnal Strings

On rainy nights she comes with a big umbrella, braving puddles in the dark as the rain falls lightly on the canopy and on the eaves of the rows of houses. Beyond the bamboo fencing, a light flickers on and off.

The priest is in his black oxfords—in fair weather he comes riding on his secondhand Phillips bicycle, and when it's pouring, he sloshes around in his black galoshes, holding a flowery girl's umbrella. Once a week he heads to the Jesuit community center, where he picks up his mail, including packages, magazines, and newspapers arriving by airmail from his native Ireland.

He brings her a pale blue rosary with a crucifix attached at the end. The night she completes the seven sacraments, the full moon looms larger than ever. He switches off the table lamp, leaving only the faint glimmer of the reading light beckoning from the nightstand.

"Come," he says.

Gaze lowered, she follows the wood-scented folds of his robe out the door. In the rippling moonlight, her heart beats faster.

The courtyard is empty. Not a soul is in sight. No streaking stray cat. No chatter.

The sound of footsteps—their footsteps—shuffles over the stepping stones. She treads softly, so softly that only one set of footsteps echoes in the dark. It grows chilly.

It is too dark to see clearly. She hears the sound of metal on metal in his fingers. Folding her arms in front, she steps back so that moonlight passes in front of her and lands on the keys.

Locating one of the longer keys, he studies it before inserting it into the keyhole, producing the scrunch of metal sliding and turning.

The scent of stale flowers wafts through the air. The pews are soaked in a soft green glow.

He lifts a corner of his robe as he steps onto the altar and switches on the candle sconce.

He approaches the carved wooden screen and, with one hand on each side, lifts it up and moves it away. He then returns and bends to move the organ stool out of the way.

He reverently straightens the folds of his robe on the wooden stool, then raises his hands as if performing a blessing and slowly removes the dark green cover.

She looks on in awe.

The arc of the wood frame glistens in the dark, with strings spread across like silvery feathers. Night light descends through the rooftop awnings and falls on the body of the harp.

Sitting at an angle with his back to her, his wavy red hair flies wild and his loose white sleeves billow. Like waves lapping at the strings of the instrument, melodic pearls burst from his fingertips.

Time stands still. As the flow touches her neck, her forehead, her chest and her back, her heart is set afloat.

A northern wind blows into this chamber of darkness, lingering like a spirit. The candlelight flickers in its wake, flickering like dark shadows.

The smattering of notes is but a prelude, a warm-up. He then proceeds to a dulcet piece, a favorite of his.

> *On a gorgeous day in April,*
> *The big ship sails past the Isle of Wight*
> *On the Ally-Ally-O...*

"My grandmother used to sing it," he says.

She tries to picture his grandmother through the hoarse yet gentle voice he must have inherited from her.

Nocturnal Strings

Ginger hair and a ruddy face, and eyes that are clear as water. A stubby old lady with round cheeks and a generous chin..

She tries hard to picture the scene. A big ship sailing out of a distant river port. A crowd is waving from afar. The Ally-Ally-O.

Then a vision of her father, mother, sister, and husband, sitting shoulder to shoulder, as if posing for a family portrait, appears in murky green lighting under the plastic awning.

Her father never came back, while her husband, likewise, disappeared.

Before she could grow up, her father went and never returned; he never met her husband.

Round, gold-rimmed spectacles on a round face, sitting in his distant study as the lattices of the window cast their shadows at his feet in front of the desk, each longer than the one before.

Dressed in his long blue gown and a black fedora, he lifts the edge of his robe to reveal the cream-colored fur lining of the lower hem. As he steps onto the footplate, he turns back and casts his gaze on them standing under the eaves.

The mule brays and the wheels of the cart begin their clickety-clack progression. Chaotic semicircular impressions are left in the snow. The wife, clinging to the shaft of the cart, moves with it. Next to the wheel tracks are the prints of a pair of once-bound feet.

On she goes until the sound of the bell dies out as the cart turns into an alley.

As temperatures rise, the shallow footprints in the snow melt into a dark, muddy slush.

It is the last she ever sees of her father.

The music stops on a single note. He plays it again and listens intently. He plucks the same string and repeats the same note. The priest stands and reaches for the frame, turning a peg at the top.

She rubs her eyes with the back of her hand.

His hand on the brim of his fedora, he peers at them from under it. He struggles onto the cart in his felt robe, with a corner exposed on the footplate. His short, stocky body quickly sinks into the cushion.

Off to Peiping. To Nanking. To Shanghai. To Hankow.

Shutting the heavy door behind her, Mother walks alone into the kitchen. A set of footprints appears in the snow-dusted courtyard.

The bell disappears into a maze of gray alleys; the fedora and felt robe gradually fade into the distance.

Resurfacing in this murky green light, he sits next to Mother, facing her with a smile on his calm, round face.

The priest lurches back into his seat. "Ally-Ally O—no, not quite right." He tries again until, finally, he heaves a sigh of relief. "Ally-Ally-O, Ally-Ally-O—now that's the way it's supposed to sound!"—as if it matters to her in the least.

The big ship sails freely again, through the murky green light, through the dark hall.

She sees herself going to school dressed as a boy. The war has begun.

Blue skies, with black bombers streaking across the sky. She helps to hang a comforter out to air between two toon trees. Her baby sister sticks her head out from inside the comforter in a game of hide-and-seek.

The planes change course and zoom away in the formation of a silver cross. The three people stand motionless in the courtyard, hands cupped over their eyes to block out the glare of the hazy sun. Not long after the mule cart leaves, the snow has nearly melted. Tufts of grass begin to grow between the shingles of the roof.

A gorgeous day in April. First the plum blossoms bloom along the south-side fence, followed by magnolias diagonally across and apricot blossoms at the head of the lane. Next come cherry-pink double petals on a row of peach trees with thick trunks by the river. The thinning morning fog drifts between flowers and barren branches. Out of the fog he appears, walking towards her, smiling and waving. Educated types are rarely trustworthy, her mother tells her. But it is love at first sight. A mist hangs above the river, obscuring the water below. No sound of flowing water, just a deafening silence. In the distance you hear the din of vehicles and soldiers approaching, wearing khakis, legs wrapped like wooden pegs. The boardwalk is narrow—she steps aside to let them through. Silently, the peach blossoms flower. It is love at first sight.

Flower after flower starts to bloom. War after war begins to erupt.

Dressed as a boy, she fights to board a train packed with fellow students. In the rear view is the courtyard strung with the drying comforter, framed by a wobbling window, as they pick up speed, racing along. The train passes through ashen plains, withered brush, and parched ranges. It comes to a stop before a bridge at nightfall, huffing and puffing billows of smoke. The lights are all out; the passengers wait in silence punctuated only by the hiss of breathing in the dark.

She presses her hand against her chest, where cash is sewn into the pocket. She is afraid to stick her head out into the pitch-black darkness. The view of the courtyard in the rear window is no more.

Fires rage in the distance. Bombers fly low overhead. Clogged streets. Congested compartments. Silent, fearful faces. Mother shuffles her once-bound feet, rushing through the courtyard. The mule lifts its foreleg. The driver raises his whip and cracks it in the air.

Wheel tracks and footprints grow ever more chaotic.

Writers often speak of war as a contest of valor, a badge of honor, their protagonists willingly racing to the killing fields to take down combatant after combatant. He jumps out of the trenches and breaks through the encirclement; a bugle sounds the notes of triumph.

But no—that's not how it is at all.

As the train silently glides past frozen rivers and starlit plains, the mother, the sister, the brick house, the courtyard, the mule cart, the tree-lined embankment, and the band of soldiers sporting thick puttees all seem to fade into the mist.

And then there's youth, school, adolescence, relationships, and much more, just as you are beginning to understand the meaning of it all.

War, oh war. Thank goodness, all wars come to an end—or so she thinks.

Fresh off the boat, she is brought to a row of Japanese wooden houses. He arrives ahead of her and is smiling and waving at her under a big banyan tree.

She knew he would be back.

He is always one to take care of business.

She sets her suitcases down on the unpaved ground at her feet, crumpling a soft, moist handkerchief in her hand. The weather is so humid she breaks into a sweat even while standing still. The prop roots of the banyan tree hang motionless in the stagnant air—he brushes them aside and walks toward her, wiping away the sweat on his brow before extending a hand.

She buys a charcoal burner from the local market, its white clay exterior accentuated with three shiny copper bands—a very pleasant look.

She props it up with a couple of bricks she finds among the weeds and sets it on the ground in front of the door.

Old newspapers are rolled up and fed into the opening at the bottom. She lights a match and uses a paper fan to gently fan the flames. Wisps of smoke rise from the thirty-six holes of the briquette. She steps back and covers her nose—it's the first time she's lit a briquette.

As she waits for the coal to gray, she rinses her rice at a public tap and mixes in red beans, then places the rice pot over the burner and allows it to simmer.

Like a loud whistle, the school bell will soon announce that school is out.

The newspaper crackles and curls, sending ashes into the air like catkins.

Soon, in the fading light of dusk, he will brush aside the prop roots of the banyan tree and walk toward her, waving and smiling.

Love, thank goodness, is worth waiting for.

Using a wooden spoon, she stirs the pot, mixing the beans evenly with the rice, as the liquid thickens. When all is ready, she will flash-fry the vegetables as he steps in the door.

At which point she hears gunfire again.

At first she thinks some family is setting off firecrackers to celebrate a special occasion. But then a military vehicle, camouflaged with netting and tree branches, rolls through her street. She rushes inside, the wooden spoon still in her hand.

With lanes so narrow, the vehicle brushes against the foliage by the front gate, snapping leaves and branches. A machine gun is mounted at the rear, manned by uniformed military police. A glimpse of their faces brings back familiar memories; the war is not yet over.

Don't go out. Back at the house, a tad later than usual, he locks the door behind him and instructs her not to go out.

In the darkness of her bedroom, she can hear the distant whistle of bullets in the air.

She pulls back her comforter and steps barefoot onto the concrete—a chill shoots up from her clenched toes. Feeling her way along the wall, she checks to see that all the doors are locked. Searchlights sweeping the area illuminate the room in flashes. She stumbles upon a hard object caught between her toes. Leaning on a chair, she lifts her foot and removes the offending article.

When she returns, she sees him curled up in bed still, seemingly sound asleep. She gently eases back into bed. Bullets burst into the alley.

"Shhh—" he turns and shushes.

People are throwing rocks at their row of houses. She begins storing up salt, sugar, and flour, placing it in separate travel-size bags.

The festive crackle of gunfire never ceases. Military drills take place at unexpected intervals in the alley, and the elementary school is closed for the time being.

He returns home silent, bringing with him bundles of newspapers, which he lays out on the table and reads alone under the kitchen lamp.

The white charcoal burner now sits behind the house, requiring a longer walk to the public tap. On a quick trip back from the market she takes note of the air raid shelters, but they're useless, open on both ends, cheaply built, good only for children to play cops and robbers in.

A rock strikes a neighbor's window, shattering the glass with a sound that pierces the ear.

A sixth-grade teacher from the school—a local woman—urges them to hide out in her mother's place overlooking the Tamsui River.

She packs a suitcase and, the very next day, just before the island is placed under martial law, travels across town with the teacher, past barbed wire fences and sandbags to a two-story building by the river. Once settled in the innermost bedroom, they lock the windows and shut the door.

They spend their days in the dark, cold as night. Every corner is damp enough to leave wet fingerprints, typical of the rainy season.

Nocturnal Strings

Amid the shriek of whistles and the thud of exploding bombs, accompanied by the rumble of vehicles rolling through the streets, gunfire like popping firecrackers turns into the sharp rat-a-tat of rapid fire.

At times the noises cease, and they can hear conversations between the teacher and her mother or other people upstairs, speaking in heavily nasal Taiwanese.

Or the sound of footsteps on wood floorboards, coming from one side, creaking to the doorway, where it stops, followed by the click of the door latch. They hold their breath.

It isn't petitioners, or political work teams, or military police.

It's only the teacher's mother inviting them out for some fresh air on the balcony. It's very late.

On dark streets, mindless gangs wander back and forth. A bonfire is lit in the near distance. Shadowy figures come their way, their faces obscured, but you can hear their footsteps. What sounds like a military detachment passes under the balcony, marching headlong into the haze. The bonfire burns quietly as the crowds return. They scale the utility poles. Power lines fall like cobwebs. The fire hydrant is removed, but no water comes out. A truck moves in—they pick up everything, toss it into the truck bed and drive away. Shadowy figures swarm back and take down doors, boards, and shop signs, tossing them into the fire, which blazes up again.

She is familiar only with the houses in front of the banyan tree; she's never been here before.

The teacher moves back to her parents' home, bringing with her newspapers for the day and the day prior for them.

"No voices deserve to be neglected," according to the paper.

From the first of the month to the second and the third, all the way to the sixth, the seventh and the eighth, bonfires continue to blaze.

They sort the papers by date and pile them on the table, looking forward to the next issue as they lose all sense of time. Searchlights sweep across the sky, shining through the frosted textured-glass windows from left to right every thirty seconds.

The sound of feet tiptoeing across the floorboards above, coming their way from the end of the hallway, then a gentle knock on the door, and they realize that it's mealtime, or maybe already dark out.

Flashes of artillery fire light up the night sky like a meteor shower, illuminating the lime-built floodgate They can't see the river. She vaguely senses the warmth of his body.

As time drags on, the first gleams of dawn appear behind the dark floodgate, releasing layer upon layer of light. The view turns warm and faintly red. A sunrise to mark the end of the rainy season.

"What a glorious day," he exclaims. They loiter a little longer before returning to the isolation of their dark room.

On March 10, in a corner of the metro section of the daily paper is a story about the drowning deaths of two young lovers who had jumped into the river after despairing of all hope, believing the current would wash their bodies out to sea, only to be swept back to the harbor at high tide to be entangled with all the other corpses.

Ever more murky waters lap against the bodies.

Water laps in dreams oblivious to boundaries between day and night. "Ah! Aayee—" he screams in his dreams. She sits up and shakes him hard.

He awakens from a deep sleep, reaches out, and holds her tight.

He flees down a tiny alley, with men in hot pursuit. He runs and runs, until he comes to a wall. Got to get over it, got to fly over that wall. But he can't. He turns into a bird and sails over the wall. No more sounds of pursuit, no more flashes of light—and all is back to normal. He is walking along a street flanked by windowless houses. Stepping on what appears to be a belt, he bends to pick up the strip of black leather. It morphs into a snake and wraps itself around his legs. He tries frantically to fly away, desperately beating his wings, only to find he has no wings! "Ahhh, ahhhh!" he screams. How terrifying. He dreams of being swallowed whole, consumed by a snake or by a quagmire.

"Look at you," she says, "you're all sweaty."

He awakens once more from the clutches of this quagmire.

This time he dreams of his father, wrapped in three layers of bedding, like sticky rice in palm leaves, floating in the surrounding harbor. Hitting up against the murky shoreline. Hitting his cold, wet feet. Encircled over and over by dark water.

"Terrifying," he says, covering his face with the comforter.

She shuts her eyes and tries hard to imagine. One day the war will be over. Everything will begin anew, start all over.

What a splendid view behind the dock. She stands beside him. A warm scent emanates from his shoulders. The trees above quietly flower. They walk on along the embankment, and, after making way for the military convoy, slowly disappear into the fog.

The bonfires grow smaller, and, one day, disappear altogether. Crowds no longer gather in the night. They walk down from the balcony and open the windows to let in fresh air.

They pack their bags and tidy up their room, not forgetting to thank their host. And back they go to the row of Japanese wooden houses.

The war is finally over, or so she believes. She moves the charcoal burner back onto the stack of bricks in the front yard.

Walking past the vendors in the local market, she considers some fabric for a new curtain. A row of barracks now stands on the grassy area behind the house, where someone appears to be peering in their direction.

She is unable to decide between a blue floral print and an orange blossom pattern, both spread out before her, both the same price.

He might prefer a brighter shade, she reasons.

But he never makes it back. Just like her father, he sets out one day and never comes home.

She waits at the door as night inches toward their little street. She lifts the rice pot from the stove and moves it into the house, taking care to wrap the top with a cloth and place the vegetables under a dome of mesh.

With daylight fading, she switches on the bare bulb hanging from the ceiling and unfurls the evening paper, spreading it out on the table. The light is dim. She reads about a young couple dressed in their Sunday best, walking hand in hand up a darkening trail to a secluded spa in the mountains, where they ingested pesticide.

She closes the newspaper, looks up at the clock, and picks out a sweater from the dresser.

Quiet, empty classrooms, one after another. No sound of children reading. Not a word written on the blackboard. Lights switched off. A lone lamp shines before the teachers' lounge.

A dark, rectangular room, with desks arranged into neat rows separated by aisles. The desks nearest to her have white name plates with black lettering in the upper right-hand corner.

His name plate is right in front of her, separated only by a pane of glass.

She raps on the glass with a knuckle, but no one answers. She walks along the corridor to the door in front. There she knocks again, but still no response. Standing under a banyan tree is a man in dark clothes, his hands in his pockets.

But she desperately wants to sit at the desk with his name on it.

The man in black starts to walk toward her.

Most likely because there is a note for you in the drawer that says what he didn't get the chance to tell you. She should have sat at the desk with his name on it.

She knocks harder. The man in black is getting closer.

She starts to retreat along the wall, slowly moving past his name plate, then bolting into a sprint.

With prop roots brushing past her face and leaves and branches scraping her skin, she dashes with ever greater speed through these dark woods. Perhaps he is already home, sitting under the lamp at the dining table, reading his paper at the table, picking up where he left off, waiting for her to return.

Spring water flows past the inn. Pesticide spills onto the tatami. "It burned a large section of the straw surface," said the boss' wife.

If only she had paid more attention to his behavior and his comments, and the company he kept. If only she'd engaged him in dinner table conversations. If only she'd asked him about work just before bed, or first thing in the morning. If only they'd gone on more outings. If only they'd had a child—not that they hadn't wanted to, but they thought there was still time.

War, oh war! Why is China embroiled in so many wars?

As the war continues to rage, she and her father, mother, and sister grow used to moving from place to place, if not living in a semi-permanent state of separation. They quietly pack up and slip away, all in complete stealth, with barely a word to each other, forever living in hiding, constantly on the run. Closing her eyes, she rests her head against the cool, vibrating walls of the bunker as bombs explode outside the shelter. One day the war will be over; everything will begin anew, start all over.

Two men in khaki tunics appear one after another to question her about his affairs. The interrogation goes on long after the barracks to the rear have played taps.

As the interrogator drones on, her mind begins to wander, settling, ultimately, on the only issue that matters: Is he back at home, or is he down in lockup?

He is dressed in long, baggy pants and black shoes. He sits cross-legged, shaking his leg to expose the gold trim on his black nylon socks and the gray hairs on his ankle and shin.

"Notice anything unusual lately?" asks Hairy Legs.

She sits straight, head down and tries hard to come up with something.

The mold in a corner of the wall expands into a crack. It reaches all the way down to the floor. Then it creeps back up in a diagonal line. It disappears behind the back of the chair.

The moldy crack turns hazy in the cigarette smoke. She searches hard for anything out of the ordinary—anything!

The train speeds ahead without a sound—you can hear the call of the plains, the flow of the river, and the rumble of the military convoy. Stagnant water; a pitch-dark compartment; the steamy breath of fellow passengers hitting her face. Bombers skim the ground. A flash of light appears in the sky, startling her awake.

Truth be told, she doesn't know a thing about him.

He's a decent man—teaches sixth grade at the local school, and never punishes his students. He heads home straight after work and enjoys a nightcap of sweet red bean porridge—that's all she knows, really.

Think harder—you have to think harder. The gray hairs on his leg poke out from the hem of his khakis. Gray newsprint ash curls into the air.

She coughs and covers her mouth with the back of her hand.

Why does everyone have to disappear?

One day she roams the streets aimlessly, pausing for neither lunch nor dinner, and doesn't return until well after dark. One day she sobs uncontrollably and reaches for a dish cloth to wipe away the tears, only to get something peppery in her eyes. She tries to rinse it out, and, in the process, forgets why she was crying.

A long line of people are waiting to move into the faculty housing she currently occupies, explains Academic Superintendent Zhang, who now sits in front of the crack in the wall. As he speaks in a drawn-out, gentle tone, it dawns on her that nothing in this world really belongs to her.

She rents a tiny room at the foot of Headwater Road, if only because it is close to work. It is menial work that a friend of a friend helped her find—not really her idea of a good job. If only she were better educated, she thinks.

The boss' wife teaches her how to use water sparingly. First wash the vegetables, then the meat, and use the same water to do the dishes—the dishes may end up a bit greasy to the touch, but don't let that bother you.

She is also taught how to chop chives. Use the spine of a knife to gather the stalks, then snip away the tough parts, and curl the fingers of the left hand as the blade comes down to chop the sprigs quickly, neatly, and safely.

The chopped chives are then mixed with oil in a large aluminum pot full of pork stuffing, which she holds in front of her, stirring vigorously with a pair of extra-long cooking chopsticks.

And when she isn't occupied with food preparation, she switches into a shirt that doesn't smell of kitchen grease and takes the bus down Roosevelt Road to the Old Town waterfront off Yanping North Road.

Tracing the shade of the floodgate, she walks along the seawall. Tufts of cogon grass grow at the foot of the thick stone wall, while water laps against the other side. The sound is somewhat distant.

Only now does she begin to appreciate the exterior of the house in the blazing sun. The gray concrete walls; the brick-red roof tiles; the imposing gates of forest green. Branches of a mimosa tree, the foliage adorned with fuzzy balls of red blossoms, reach out above the gate.

She looks up and sees the second-story balcony.

She goes from task to task, with no breaks in between. She is so dependable; the boss turns everything over to her, while he relaxes upstairs.

She arrives early in the morning, removes the two planks used to board up the entrance, and props up the shade sail with a metal pole. She then puts on her slate-blue apron and retrieves the cooking chopsticks, the stirring spoon, and the funnel. One of these days, she tells herself, she's going to open a much classier joint than this.

The first rays of dawn are filtered through the wispy smoke rising from the stove. She sees her mother, a skilled baker, sitting alone at the large square table. The warm light of the bulb beneath the beaded lampshade casts a yellow tinge on one side of her face and on the bare arm lying on the tabletop. As the light dims, she dozes off. The next day she sees her mother again, this time with her hair combed, using a fire poker to remove dough starter from the oven. She holds the dough, still piping hot, between her fingers. As she blows on the yeasty dough, ashes mixed with hot steam escape past both sides of her face, dancing in the morning's early light.

The figure with the black fedora is long gone.

The sound of the bell on the mule cart resonates from the end of some invisible street.

He sits up, sweating profusely as he leans his head against a bedpost, telling her the story of his father—this after the second nightmare.

Tall and muscular, he was an army medic who fell victim to typhoid during the war. He was sent home wrapped in three layers of bedding, his long legs sticking out from the rear of the mule cart, jolting every time there was a bump in the road. Not long after, he was carted out, this time with his head jutting out, his body wrapped in military burlap.

A black-and-white portrait of the deceased sat in the wicker shopping basket carried back and forth from the market. It sat on a kitchen shelf. The portrait smiled down on the family at mealtime.

They had a little brown dog, a stray he rescued from the army clinic. The dog later drowned in a well in the courtyard. Neighbors dumped a large pack of powdered alum into the well—for days the water fizzled with bubbles.

He recounts too his childhood friends and their favorite pastimes. The village candy store, the fruit vender. A carpentry shop and a brick factory under the bridge.

Now awake, he sits up straight and tells his story with his arms tucked under the comforter.

She listens.

The lattices of the windows cast ever longer shadows as a man sits slouched in his study, next to a woman around a large square table. Rays filtered through the beaded lampshade cast a yellow glow on the sides of their faces, and on the bare arms they rest on the tabletop.

They exchange words, little of which can be made out. There is occasional movement in their yellow-tinged limbs.

The light dims; the room grows darker. The light flickers as fireflies come to the mosquito net shared with her sister. They open the netting and a warm breath blows onto their faces.

A comforter hangs between two toon trees, while her sister crouches between the folds. "Come out," shouts the mother from afar. "Come out or you're in for a spanking!" The comforter turns and moves; peonies bloom in full glory.

Felt Fedora gestures good-bye. Gold-rimmed glasses glint under the brim of the hat in the glare of the melting snow. Gray newsprint ash floats up to the green roof tiles. Wisps of smoke rise from the thirty-six holes of the briquette. The gray-haired calf is shaking.

Ten days earlier she did not know a thing; ten days later she has learned about his childhood. But wouldn't it be odd to tell Hairy Legs about the father, or tell him about the little brown dog? He'd say she was crazy.

But what does it matter? Once he's told her about his childhood, he's gone. How he meets his fate matters little, for once he's gone he'll cease to make a difference. For people, nothing changes just because you're gone—

A corner of the felt robe hangs outside the cart; the entwined legs of the lovers on the tatami jut out beyond the *shoji* screen; the father's head, wrapped in burlap, dangles over the edge of the cart.

He cannot recall the fourth line after "a gorgeous day in April." Mother and kid sister are still in the north country. The grandmother, who must be over a hundred now, calls from the quayside.

She was so eager for him to join the clergy, whereas his ambition was to become a resident harpist at an inn.

The Ally-Ally-O, the Ally-Ally-O, The big ship again sails through the harbor, sailing over dark, icy rivers. In the green glow, he smiles and waves at her. The ship sails toward the harp's feathery strings.

She was certain he'd be back. She was so sure.

After the curtains are hung, she'd buy a table and some good chairs. The little room facing the barracks can be converted into a study. The bonfires would cease and the demonstrations die down, and they could focus on starting a family.

Surely he feels the same way—or so she thinks.

She may have been reluctant at first and might have hesitated to answer. But, if he had asked, she would ultimately have agreed to go with him. He knew this.

She had believed that once the war was over, all would return to normal—but who'd have expected that when it all ended, it would drag everything down with it?

It was the war that had brought them together; now she was actually nostalgic for the war years.

Fires raging outside the wall; people shouting here and there; the river's dark waters lapping against the floodgate, enveloped by uncertainty in the darkness.

He feels his way in the dark and affectionately puts his arm around her waist and draws her near. The air is damp. Between their hushed heavy breathing she picks up from the nape of his neck a familiar arboreal scent.

When it is over, he tucks the comforter neatly around her neck and holds her hand under the covers, reaching around her head to caress her cheek with the back of the other hand.

The room lights up in a hazy glow as the flash of artillery fire beams through the frosted textured-glass window. Every thirty seconds or so, they look over at each other.

He actually brought up the issue.

He actually brought it up—during those ten nights and days they spent together, in that dank room where the river lapped against the foot of the bed, as he gently caressed her cheek in the quiet of the night, all their questions, all their intimations, all their deliberations, and all their struggles unfolded amid pain and desperation.

He then made up his mind—for her sake, he explained.

The music winds down, devolving from the stirring climax to a low, inaudible moan. It settles into irretrievable time, where all is dark save for a faint light illuminating the oblong chancel.

Spring water trickles onto the wooden dome of the church, onto the second-story tiled roof, onto the courtyard, into the well. The wet carcass of the little brown dog is fished up out of the well; no tears are shed—the spectators simply walk away. The carpentry shop and brick factory have been demolished. The mule cart creaks off into the distance.

His voice begins to strain, and he stops singing. An echo reverberates from afar.

The elementary school is in session. School-age children emerge from nearby alleys. Crossing guards arrive at the school office, where they pin on red armbands with black lettering, retrieving long batons from behind the lockers and stepping out onto the crosswalk. "Stop!" When they hold out their batons, traffic and pedestrians alike come to a halt. Students form an orderly line at the intersection and start striding across: "One-two, one-two…"

The shrill of a whistle marches in from the tiled roofs of Wenzhou Street, carrying with it an unfinished tune, to quaysides where a father's body lies afloat and lovers entangle in an embrace, and to the home of a grandmother.

Ten long days, with daylight hours indistinguishable from night. A border town in the north, winter clothes airing in a courtyard. A comforter with flowering peonies. Walls of white chalk. Roofs with grass sprouting between the shingles. A turtle dove perching on a father's hand. A short stubby finger pushing down against the lower lip; a loud whistle sailing across the sky.

Ireland—what a faraway place!

Glancing at the flame of the stove and the noodles turning in boiling water, she curls her fingers and begins to slice the meat.

It isn't until the customers are all gone that she begins to lose focus, with mist in her eyes like someone in love for the first time, whose story has yet to conclude.

A man in a navy blue coat pushes open the door. He sits alone at a table in the corner. Shoulders hunched, he exhales a warm breath of air and rubs his palms.

She places a portion of noodles in the skimmer and dips it into the bubbling pot.

She grabs a dash of chopped scallions from a dish on the shelf, sprinkles it over the spread of meat slices, and serves it piping hot to her patron.

He looks up and smiles as he takes the bowl and brings it close. He then moves his chair closer to the table and picks a pair of chopsticks from the bamboo holder.

At this hour there is no traffic—all is quiet save for the tap of bamboo on porcelain, and the slurping of noodles. A gecko with a broken tail slips out from behind the counter and quietly sits at the edge of the wall.

There is the hint of a resemblance in the profile.

For him to appear out of the blue and pretend to order a bowl of noodles like a customer, casually slurping his noodles, allowing her to slowly discover his presence, introducing an element of surprise—isn't completely out of the realm of possibility.

He blows on the steamy noodles, then pulls a white handkerchief from his pocket to wipe his nose.

Out of the mists of early spring his face appears, smiling as he walks toward her.

She returns the aluminum lid to the boiling cauldron. The steam dissipates. The gecko now hangs upside down from the ceiling.

After wiping his face and hands, he stands and puts on his jacket.

A cold wind blows in as opens the door to leave.

She gives each surface another wipe. The chairs are placed upside-down on the tables.

The aluminum pot with leftover noodles is laid on the floor as she locks up. The clang of metal reverberates through the quiet street. She gives the gate another tug to make sure it is locked before letting the padlock fall heavily against the door.

The neon lamps emit a reddish glow, dyeing her body red as she walks past lamppost after lamppost. With both hands, she gingerly balances the handles of the stock pot, for fear the liquid will spill onto her shoes.

"Let me help you with that!"

The sound of a familiar voice.

A warm brush of the shoulder.

She was certain he'd be back.

Hesitatingly, she hands over the pot. As his hand touches hers, warmth spreads.

"How have you been all these years?" he asks.

"Ahem," she answers, gaze turned downward. That is as much as she is willing to say, still cross with him.

He reaches out and touches her waist. She blushes, turning red in the dark.

That was a good ten years ago.

She pauses and turns around, where a quiet street stretches out before her, soaked in the red of a streetlamp. The street is empty save for herself and the tall, slender shadows of regularly spaced lampposts.

She rests the pot handle on her hip, freeing one hand to smooth her hair, then reaches down for the handle. The plastic soles of her shoes again squeak like chirping insects.

Standing in the darkness of Headwater Road, she senses a chill in the air, rising from the end of the street. This, they say, is where they used to execute prisoners a decade ago.

6

CRUELTY OF THE CITY

Walis Nokan
(translated by Edward Vickers)

Missing Pieces

Only one road winds its way up the mountain to the Kobu Settlement behind Taoyuan's Fuxing Township. The road is all but hidden amid the abundant high-altitude honey peach trees and, in May, a carpet of peach blossoms. I once spent a week across from the home of a friend, Ma Shao, at the top, where the road ended. I recall it was shortly before December, for the image my memory displays is one of pervasive mist over the Kobu Settlement, barely visited by the sun's rays. I was just finishing up my fieldwork.

At about the time darkness took over from the remaining daylight, an old man emerged from the tin shack down below, stripped to the waist. On the patch of open ground beside his home he then performed what, to someone of my generation, was a dated calisthenics routine:

the "Imperial Subjects' Exercises for National Construction," mandatory in all upper middle schools during the colonial era. After exercising for half an hour, his skin glistening with misty sweat, he retrieved his clothes from the bare branches of a nearby peach tree, dressed himself, and reentered his shack.

Moments later, strains of a piano rippled through the vast empty space. I could hardly express my astonishment at hearing such rare and precious sounds, a piano playing classical music nurtured by European culture. I recall that the pianist concluded with Beethoven's Fifth Symphony in E-minor, the "Symphony of Fate," whose thundering opening chords seemed to shake the withered leaves off the surrounding trees. But the old man faltered at the finale, allowing broken chords to cascade down the mountainside into the Takekan Creek below.

One day, I summoned up the courage to approach the tin shack, only to find the door shut fast, a rusty lock barring the way to the piano and its elderly player. Perhaps, I thought, he performed his solitary exercises, both physical and musical, after returning home late each evening from his distant orchard. Such a pattern of life recalled the reclusive hermits of a bygone era.

On the last day of the week, that stage of my fieldwork now complete, I arrived in front of the tin shack, where I stood staring, hoping for some sort of miracle. What fell from the heavens was no miracle, but a drenching, icy mountain downpour. I hastened downhill, the torrential rain almost washing me headlong into the valley below.

Standing at the Kobu bus stop, bursting with curiosity, I asked the waiting tribespeople for information about the man in the tin shack:

"Ever heard the sound of a piano here in the valley?"

"Oh, sure! We've all heard that. It's like the music of a violent storm in a forest!"

"Have you ever seen the player?"

"Of course, we have. He plays an 'air piano,' but we still like the way it sounds."

"Why 'air piano'? Is there no actual instrument?"

Not just no piano, but no fingers to play it with; he lost all ten!"

"His fingers ?"

"They were all chopped off at the Garrison Command. What a shame. He was our great musical talent!"

"Would you take me to see him?"

"See him? What are you talking about? Watan passed away more than thirty years ago! Your brains are like a rotting camphor tree."

Watan, it turned out, was a tribal musician who had fallen victim to the White Terror of the 1950s. His case remained unreported, part of our buried past. And so, to this day, my fieldwork remains incomplete, like a puzzle missing some pieces.

Blame It All on the Bronze Statue
Our small town wakes up early. When the sun is still hiding beneath its mountain bedclothes, as if reluctant to face a new day, the town is already stretching and stirring. If it weren't for the thick tin rooftops, the hawkers at the market alone would turn the town upside down.

Home to fewer than a hundred thousand people, Heping stands on a plateau hemmed in on three sides by mountains. To the south, a new six-lane highway leads straight to a big city. Worried about growth, our township chief ignored the Health Bureau's "Two Children, Just Right!" campaign. Raising the banner of ideas by experts and scholars, he announced at an assembly at the township's public middle school: "Research by experts has determined that, by the year 2000, our country will confront the problem of an aging population, and the effects of this on our national development (er uh . . .), especially on the development of our own town, will be severe. And so, as your chief, I encourage everyone to do their utmost to raise the birth rate for the sake of the nation! . . . Er, what I mean is, as township chief, I urge you, once you've all grown up, to have lots of babies. Now, of course, you must follow propriety in relations between the, ah, sexes. You all agree, don't you?"

Below the podium, the enthusiastic clapping by those from the Office of Student Affairs finally managed to stir the audience into thunderous applause. The school custodian, Old Liu, who had been dozing behind the podium, was jolted awake; imagining himself caught up in the rapturous reception of the Great Leader's speech, he hurriedly joined in the applause, energetically exercising his withered hands as he had not done for twenty, no, thirty years. Alone in the bare backstage room, he continued the explosion of sound—so resounding, so melodious! Old Liu was reveling in the "great atmosphere" he had created!

The youngsters sitting primly in the audience ran out of patience. Several boys were sizing up some of the "hot" girls; one was practicing martial arts moves on the back of the head of the girl in front, and, of course some were embellishing the applause with strings of obscenities—"Fuck! Fuck! Fuck!"—safe in the knowledge that they could not be heard from the stage and could vent their unhappiness over being "imprisoned" in the auditorium. Both sides got what they wanted.

The assembly concluded; the dignitaries exited the stage and made good their escape. The unfortunate students, however, had to sing the school song and chant slogans, as if declarations of lifelong loyalty were the price of their release.

As they were leaving the hall, Old Liu posted himself in front of the bronze statue to take their salutes as they filed past. It was a school rule that all students passing the statue must make a three-fingered salute as a sign of respect. To violate this regulation was to insult the former head of state. No sooner had this rule been promulgated than the statue seemed to have become a restricted area, exemplifying the old adage "Venerate gods and demons from a distance!" Students would chart circuitous routes around the auditorium to avoid paying obeisance when school was out, even if it meant trekking dozens of meters out of their way. Trouble was, they had to pass by the statue on their trips to and from the auditorium for Monday assemblies.

Old Liu was wise to such tricks and quick to detect the students' lack of enthusiasm. Like Mao Sui volunteering to serve the King of Chu, he begged the student affairs officer to allow him to undertake the "vital duty" of enforcing proper respect. He proposed that before and after each weekly assembly he would stand before the statue, so that he could inform on any "unpatriotic elements" who came to his notice. And so every Monday morning, at exactly ten-past eight and again at nine o'clock, residents of Heping Township saw a figure standing silently to attention, like a statue beside the statue.

According to the testimony of Old Liu's wife (a Cantonese woman who ran Stall Number Eight in Heping's Number One Market, serving soy milk at breakfast, and Taiwanese noodles in soup in the evening), her husband was fanatically devoted to this "vital duty," or, more precisely, to the precious statue. "I have undergone ten thousand trials and, with foresight, tirelessly plotted and planned to secure just such a position! Just think! From now on, every cohort of graduates from this school will have saluted me at least 240 times! Can you imagine the glory of receiving such adulation from the masses?" As the Cantonese woman related her husband's words, it was almost as if she, too, saw herself taking on the statue's persona. At such times, her face had a timely glow that was different from what emanated from the thick metal skin.

Were you to treat Old Liu as some sort of psychological case study, I guarantee you'd feel obliged to rake over the traces of his childhood painstakingly. Alternatively, you might want to attempt hypnosis to force him to reveal, bit by bit, the dramatic story of his exploits battling Communist bandits and the Japanese, to substantiate scholarly logical reasoning; but Liu was not someone you could approach easily. Most likely, his deep-rooted revolutionary ideas would lead to a meandering, pointless quarrel. It would be much like the forced debates of the always feckless Legislative Yuan.

Let us therefore forget that rather worthless suggestion, and instead rely on the more primitive approach of observing his daily life.

Old Liu is now busy accepting the "homage of the masses." Determined to assume a befittingly dignified and reverent appearance, he maintains a "stony" expression. Based on the latest theatrical interpretation, "stony" means that not even a dog walking by will smile. This was evidently the posture Old Liu maintained.

But this stony posture of his in front of the statue attracted a different sort of formulation from certain little devils among the students. Having discovered that Old Liu was from Guangdong, they postulated that no dog would feel inclined to smile at the canine stench of a dog-eating Cantonese. This, at least, was the interpretation on campus of his stony demeanor.

Of course, the "official view" of Old Liu on the part of the school authorities was that he was nothing more than a guard—that is, um, a dedicated worker and a loyal, patriotic party member. This was precisely how the eminent principal put it at a school affairs meeting, citing the custodian as an exemplary patriot. Liu overheard this praise while pouring tea for the assembled hardworking teachers, and that took him back forty years, to when he had devoted himself wholeheartedly to fight the enemy. His tea-pouring right hand shook uncontrollably from gratitude at receiving such recognition; he was so touched that his veins swelled. As a result, forty-six teachers found the edges of their teacups stained yellow-brown by tea.

However, by only the thirteenth performance of his salute-taking ritual before the statue, Old Liu was already experiencing a nagging sense of boredom. The students were so adept at faking that he had yet to see any results from his important and sacred mission of earning glory for the school showing loyalty to the party that was displaying filial piety to the country by ridding the people of a scourge. Unable to report any unpatriotic individuals to the school authorities, he feared he'd be thought lazy and unproductive. If this situation worsened, he imagined a sad fate awaiting him: "You're fired!"

In the following weeks, he kept a careful watch, not only observing whether each student saluted but also "how" they saluted, in the hope of detecting even a minuscule lapse in protocol. For only then could he demonstrate loyalty to the party filial piety to the country and commitment to ridding the people of a scourge. He fervently wished he could sprout ten—a hundred—no, a thousand extra eyes to fulfil his mission! Regrettably, however, the students were simply too smart for him. In other words, the school's "saluting training" was one hundred percent successful.

As the first semester drew to a close, having failed to score any "combat points," his routine degenerated to this extent—he would use three to five minutes of the ten he spent standing by the statue resting with his eyes closed, recalling various delightful scenarios. A little daydreaming is harmless, he reassured himself. In the previous year, he had hidden behind bushes to monitor the entire statue perimeter. Occasionally, students intent on their play strayed into the "forbidden zone," but they would invariably follow the rules and salute the statue.

Meanwhile, the teachers, the directors, even the principal himself, when they passed the statue, never made the slightest gesture of respect, breezing by as if they hadn't seen it. When he first noticed their behavior, Liu experienced an unprecedented conflict, so unbearable he felt himself on fire, evoking emotions he had felt when fleeing the mainland thirty-eight years before. It was only when he heard, over the school PA system, the Kuomintang propaganda song "There's a National Flag in My Heart" that the conflict dissipated. Then he was overcome with admiration for the profound patriotism of all the staff: to have the national flag flying *in* your heart; this was the supreme expression of national sentiment! No wonder that, on passing before the statue, there was no need on their part for any formal manifestation.

"They're so much better than me," said Old Liu to himself.

"So much better!"

As soon as these words escaped his yellowing teeth, he slowly opened his eyes, dragging himself from contemplation of those delightful scenes back to reality. He should have kept his eyes shut, for, when the puffy lids opened, wow! Unbelievable. It was just as Mencius had written, "Those upon whom Heaven has bestowed a great mission must first suffer and strive." And Old Liu told himself, "I am indeed a man capable of fulfilling a great duty!" Having stood sentinel for an entire semester, today, at last, he had caught two "unpatriotic" students red-handed! Or was he dreaming? He decided to bite down hard on the second finger of his right hand—the very digit he'd once used to pull the trigger on those Communist bandits! Ow! That hurt! His teeth might be old, but they were still strong!

"Stop right there, you!"

He yelled at them, like a military commander. They froze in confusion, unaware of the scope of the disaster that had befallen them.

Old Liu lost no time in marching the two miscreants to the Office of Student Affairs on the second floor. One of the them had turned deathly pale from fright. The typical look of a criminal playing for sympathy, the custodian thought.

The director's door was ajar, but, unable to suppress his enthusiasm and anxious to secure credit, he marched into the office, exclaiming, "I've caught them, Sir!"

Talking to oneself in an empty office is a sure sign of a mental short-circuit. One of the students could not suppress a snigger.

"What! You dare laugh at me! We'll see who feels like laughing in a minute! At least one major demerit for each of you. Damn it! Insulting our Leader!"

The outburst over, Old Liu stepped back out into the corridor. On hearing "one major demerit for each of you," the students finally realized the gravity of their situation.

"Yibu, what are we gonna do?"

The two Atayal boys from a mountain village north of town had just arrived at the school, where they were assigned to the first grade. All this was new to them.

"How should I know?"

The student who had sniggered was befuddled, unaware of the nature of the terrible crime he'd committed. But "insulting the leader" was not an offense to be taken lightly.

"Yibu, why did the custodian bring us here? What does it mean to 'insult the leader'? Is this going to be like those times when our Atayal elders take us into the forest to search for plants we're not familiar with?"

This student was called Hayung. The settlement children had given him a nickname which meant "the little mouse who's never seen a wild boar," no doubt in tribute to his timidity.

"Don't be stupid! Your father wasted money sending you to school. You need to 'learn how to find the road to a palm civet.' You've got a dictionary in your bag, why don't you use it? 'Insulting the leader' is the mistake we just made, not saluting the custodian."

In the tone of an adult admonishing a child, Yibu scolded Hayung to show that he was a cut above his friend.

"How was I supposed to know that not saluting the custodian meant 'insulting the leader'? Yibu, back there when I had my head down, thinking of my sick mama as I walked along; you should have warned me! You call yourself a friend?"

Hayung vented his anger, as if the fact that he was made to stand there awaiting punishment was all Yibu's doing.

"Sharing troubles is what real friends do. The fact that I'm standing here with you should make you grateful to have a friend like me instead of getting mad!"

Yibu's rebuke was cut short by a sound from the corridor. They could hear Old Liu's cry: "Director! Sir! I have just apprehended two unpatriotic students!" They could almost see the three-foot trail of spittle from Liu's mouth.

"Good work, Old Liu! Good work! The higher-ups will definitely reward you well for this. Very well done indeed!"

"Thank you, thank you for your kind words, Director!"

A moment later, Yibu and Hayung were alone with the director, who sat before them on the sofa in his light, airy office.

"Your names?" The director glowered, like a predator sizing up its prey. The boys' Atayal fathers wore a similar expression when they ventured into the forest on a hunting expedition.

"Hayung," "Yibu," they answered, without hesitation, terrified that one word or movement could provoke the wrath of this fearsome adversary.

"What have you two been learning at school? Can't you speak Mandarin?"

The boys had miscalculated. Like animals caught in a well-laid trap, the more they struggled, the more frightened they became.

"Chen Jimin!"

"Yang Guangchuan!" came their replies, like the wails of two wild animals.

"Mountain people, aren't you?" said the Director, looking irritated.

"Yes." Yibu, a.k.a. Chen Jimin, felt he needed to speak up for poor Hayung and instill some confidence.

As the director spoke, he shifted his body, blocking the room's only window, as if to keep important secret dealings about to transpire within from ears coming in on the wind.

"Yibu—er, I mean, Chen Jimin—just said we insulted the leader because we didn't salute the custodian. Something like the tribal concept of gaga for us Atayal people: when we've done something wrong, we have to be punished."

Timid Hayung, it seemed, had finally acquired the brave heart of a hunter, but, as if he were seeking Yibu's approval, his neck turned automatically toward his friend.

Yibu nodded vigorously:

"We know we've done something bad!"

"What? You think you're in trouble because you didn't salute Old Liu?"

They wondered why a hunter who had his prey firmly in his grasp would still be angry. They'd already admitted they'd screwed up.

"Yes, so the custodian got mad and dragged us up here."

Yibu, with the spirit of a child of the mountains, took pride in his bravery in answering. He assumed that Hayung, after all, was "the little mouse who's never seen a wild boar," and could never be reckoned his equal.

"Tell me," said the director, pointing his finger at ashen-faced Hayung. "What is the thing behind where Old Liu was standing?"

Hayung considered for a moment, before cautiously answering, "A statue."

"Yes, a statue. You should salute that statue because it is the statue of our honored former President Chiang. Didn't your teachers tell you that?"

As the director uttered the five words "our honored former President Chiang," he jumped to his feet and stood at attention. Terrified by this sudden movement, Yibu and Hayung both took a step backward. Like a deflated balloon, the director promptly sank back into his chair.

Yibu and Hayung could not understand why the failure to salute a statue might constitute such a grave transgression. They never had such a ritual in their settlement primary school. There, the most that was expected of them was to stand for the national anthem. Of course, they were also expected to bow to the school principal and the teachers. But they had never heard of saluting a "thing" like a statue. If they weren't mistaken, being made into a statue meant you were dead, someone who, as the textbooks put it, had "become an ancient." How could homage paid by the living to the dead be an expression of patriotism? For a moment, Yibu was tempted to contradict the director, but the man was acting like a raging wild boar. Yibu well knew that, if unarmed and confronted with an enraged boar, one's best option was to hide or, more accurately, run for it. So, swallowing his indignation, he kept his questions to himself.

As for Hayung, suffering this unprovoked injury seemed to have made him even more fearful than usual. He was generally the first of his classmates to bow in respect on encountering any teachers, directors, or the school principal. He was convinced that only rituals like saluting could protect his timid heart. But a nagging question troubled his young head: Was worrying about his sick old mama less important than saluting the statue of a dead man? Needless to say, fear prevented him from putting this query to the director.

For Old Liu, Heping's guardian of the statue, accomplishment of this one heroic act seemed to restore, in one stroke, the lost-long dignity from before, during the early years of displacement. He could hold himself as straight-backed and upright as the military police in front of the Presidential Palace. Moreover, he now conducted his inspections mornings and evenings, sometimes even climbing a ladder to the top of the statue, where, sitting on its neck, he would gently wipe away the accumulated dust and debris from the crown, ears, and nose. He sometimes muttered to himself and shed a few loyal tears. It was an oddly moving spectacle.

We can understand why Old Liu the custodian loved, adored, and doted on that statue by what his Cantonese wife said he told her at the market. "Now," he declared, "I am a school celebrity! Apart from my lifelong loyalty to the party, love for the motherland and dedication to protecting the masses, my greatest contribution lies above all in guarding the statue! It's been my greatest honor to serve the statue of so great a man! So please stop nagging me for patrolling all the time. Without that statue, I wouldn't be here; and without me, you'd be a widow."

Two weeks after the two Atayal students were given demerits over the statue, we were astonished to find Old Liu paralyzed with grief, weeping inconsolably at the foot of the statue. A prankster had poured a tin of green paint onto the effigy's head, leaving green scars on the bronze flesh from the head down. A total disaster. Heping Township found itself at the center of a media storm, and the people were in a state of high anxiety. According to newspaper reports, the most likely culprit was an opposition party firebrand, since a statue elsewhere had recently been pulled down. The following night, no one would have dreamed that Yibu would be furiously scrubbing off the pungent smell of paint with soap. How unpleasant it must have been to wash with cold water so late at night.

(This story is purely fictitious. Any similarity to actual events is entirely coincidental and a product of the will of Heaven.)

Formosan Landlocked Salmon
I recall that dark shadows often flitted over his face, as if catching dappled shadows cast by the mountain trees. We were on a small farm 1,600 meters above sea level, near a tributary of the Dajia River. Branching off

the route from the Qingshan Power Plant was a road built by the Japanese during the colonial era when they sought to open up the country and control the local tribes. Three kilometers from the junction, the road passed through a steep-sided, narrow gorge that had clearly been hewn out of the rock by hand; only a small 1600cc automobile could gain access. After driving past the wooden gate of an abandoned guard post, we reached the farm, hidden in the rarely frequented depths of the forest.

To the Tafulan Atayal, he was known as "Bota's son," meaning that he was an Atayal from Fuxing Township to the north. According to the legend of the Fuxing Atayal, Bota was the great hero of the tribal migration. He was who had driven the Smayun from the lands above the Shimen Reservoir, and it was said that the blood from his warriors' knives made the river flow red as far as the Taipei Basin.

The greatest mystery of this smallholding must be the landlocked Formosan salmon in the stream. Unfortunately, they are fish with an attitude, generally thought to be confined just to this Qijiawan Creek. The salmon here are never sold to outsiders, and the Atayal themselves do not eat them. It used to be that central government officials were served this delicacy when they came on an inspection tour or stopped by to visit the creek. On such occasions, the fish that graced the banquet table would come from none other than this stream.

In truth, I am not particularly interested in the Formosan salmon. What interests me are the myths and legends of the Tafulan people. This farm is on Tafulan ancestral territory, and it was here that Chief Hayung farmed and watched over his forefathers' lands. The Tafulan say that, around thirty years before, a northerner arrived and managed to acquire this land in an extraordinary manner: he sold a secret to the chief.

To this day, no one knows what that secret was. There was one occasion when Losin, a trusted aide of the chief, got drunk and let slip a hint, saying that "Bota's son" spoke up for the tribe. He had been interrogated and tortured by the Garrison Command, but as if his mouth had been sewn shut, he revealed nothing. "If anyone tries to push me around," Losin had said emphatically, "I'll dump him into the Dajia River!"

In checking various material, I came across the last documented case, dated 1973, when a school principal in Fuxing Township was accused of fomenting revolt by organizing a local youth team. To this day, I still recall how his voice trembled, his air of book-learning making him seem cold and detached, as it lacked the convivial warmth typical of the Atayal. When we were done talking, right before I left, my last impression about the place was a gray pall and darkness against a sky bereft of sparkling stars. It was a rare evening scene, not normal in September.

Climbing up to Siyuan Mountain Pass from the Dazhuoshui River one reaches "a beautiful land brimming with deer antlers," my favorite description, during my fieldwork days, for Huanshan, also known as Sooyaw. Passing Mount Li, I recalled the tales told by the Tafulan; it would be interesting to encounter a northerner here, in the mountains of central Taiwan. Parking my car at the guard post, I took a shaded path along a small stream, its bed clearly visible through the limpid water. Here the symmetrical, speckled salmon could be seen cavorting, unperturbed by the arrival of a stranger.

The owner, in contrast, looked surprised. I explained that I was staying nearby and was fond of researching the history of migration among the mountain tribes. The farmer was not a young man. "It's good to study the past," he observed, re-emerging from his hut with a small flask of rice liquor. Sitting on a bench of felled wood, he poured a cup of wine and offered it to me, shaking his head thoughtfully: "But not entirely good..."

His small farm, surrounded by the trees, felt to me like a lake, all sorts of intruding noises swallowed up by its still waters. Even our subdued voices roused the serene forest. To the north, the Xueshang Range stood like raised swords, sunlight no longer glinting off the blades. After a few cups, my muscles loosened and my thoughts felt like drifting clouds. I was bold enough to praise the old man for his brave refusal to betray the tribe, even under threat of torture. He froze for a moment, cup in hand. It was then that I first saw an indescribable shadow flit across his countenance, though I thought it was the swaying of tree shadows. I sobered up at once, sensing I should slink away before my host lost his temper.

Instead, he seemed to recover and drained the cup he was holding. Far from displaying anger, he heaved a long sigh, as if feeling liberated.

"Son, would you like to hear the story of the Formosan salmon?"

I happily agreed, whereupon he added a condition that sounded easy but would be hard to carry out: "When I've finished my story, how you write it down is up to you."

The following is what I wrote. He spoke mainly in Mandarin, occasionally slipping into Atayal and Japanese—a mix of languages that, at that time, was rare.

It was around 1950. Back then, I was younger than you are now. In Beifeng District, a group of intellectuals from the mountain tribes were planning a campaign for autonomy (in the early Nationalist period, Beifeng was north of a line connecting Nan'ou Township and Wufeng Township in present-day Hsinchu). This was led by enlightened elders from the colonial period, including Losin Watan, who later changed his name to Lin Ruichang, a relative of my father's generation. Losin Watan was a political advisor to the provincial government. Youngsters like us were mostly students in teacher's colleges.

It's strange to think of it now, but at the time we would often congregate in the library in the basement of the museum in Taipei's New Park, where there was a large collection of books in Japanese. It was as if we were all competing to absorb the new knowledge, feeling that only in this way could we become "new youth" ready to face the challenges of the age. We read *Capital* by Marx and Engels, Adam Smith's *Wealth of Nations*, and the philosophy of Hegel and Kant. Hard to believe, isn't it? But all these works passed freely across our desks. Bacon said that knowledge is power, and we were convinced that the combination of knowledge and a popular movement would lead to a great revolution. We were all believers in the theory of class struggle. Among our comrades, some became revolutionary martyrs, others were jailed for "thought crimes," while those who survived either persisted in silence or abandoned their socialist ideals.

In Taipei, there was a Mountain Regions Guesthouse dating from the Japanese period, since renamed the Mountain Regions Native-Place Hall, and this was where we often gathered to talk about things. I clearly recall that one member of our group was a teacher from Gaoyi, in Fuxing Township, called Teimu Shiad, who was a few years older than the rest of us. He was our senior at the Normal School. One Saturday afternoon he stormed in holding a communist pamphlet and began venting his dissatisfaction with all our theorizing about tribal autonomy, which appealed to a gentle emotionalism. The dark patina on his face, suggesting liver problems stemming from overexertion, left a deep impression on me. His most off-putting feature was his dwarfish, coarse appearance: when seated, he looked like a heap of tumbled thatch; when he stood to voice criticism, he had the air of a trapped wild boar. He insisted that, in the absence of armed revolution, the self-determination movement was mere romantic bourgeois fantasy. The dissemination of knowledge is time-consuming and difficult; the masses must be aroused by heated passion, and intellectuals are the sighting device for this massive weapon of passion. I did not completely agree with him, but his ardent intensity astounded me. What made the deepest impression was not so much his argument as his demonic tone and terrifying charisma, which both frightened and delighted me, recalling the image of Hitler, who had recently died.

We were at the rear railway station, where we stopped as usual for a bowl of hot noodles before going our separate ways. Just then, several local toughs emerged from a dark alley, and I remember one of them spitting out; "Huh! Even dead savages eat noodles!" We all rushed to get away, except Teimu, who was slumped in his seat, so frightened that he threw up, littering the table with a mess of slimy, yellow noodle fragments.

Over the following months, Lin Ruichang, our enlightened leader, occasionally brought along a stranger, a scruffily dressed man from Tangshan who would always sit with a smile and listen to us sound off. At moments like this, Teimu Shiad sounded like an orator or someone at a guidance session; but while he appeared to have forgotten that cowardly display of vomiting at the noodle stall, none of us could forget it.

Later, we learned that this stranger from Tangshan had been sent by the Provincial Mountain Work Committee. Lin Ruichang and elders of the Tsou tribe around Alishan had already been arrested. The wave of arrests by the secret police crashed over us like a violent storm, and an unspeakable stillness descended on the mountain villages. By that time, thanks to careful arrangements made by Teimu, most of us had been posted to various mountain primary schools, which felt like safe havens. The plans to establish a Penglai Tribal Self-help Campaign Alliance, about which we had fantasized for so long, were indefinitely put on hold. The simple declarations and crude graphics, as well as the romanized Atayal script we had developed, were entrusted to Teimu for safekeeping. Since he had been promoted to director at his school, his position seemed safer than ours.

In the spring of 1952, a telephone call at school instructed me to attend a study session in the Three People's Principles. At the door I was seized by two plainclothes policemen. At the police headquarters, I was placed in solitary confinement with a confession and a ballpoint pen on the floor. I knew something had gone wrong.

Determined to remain faithful to my revolutionary principles, I kept my lips sealed. Of course, this earned me relentless and extremely painful beatings. The incessant torture made me lose track of time. I was transferred to the Jingmei Detention Center, where almost all the teachers from the mountain villages who shared my views ended up. For a whole month, we were physically and spiritually drained, like dying fish gasping for water on a fishmonger's slab, our days an alternating succession of faintings, dousings, stabbing pain, and brief snatches of troubled sleep.

When I thought that the jailers believed I had passed out again, I heard whispering, like the buzzing of happy bees: "Is this one of them?" "Yes!" The informer's voice sounded familiar. I struggled to open my swollen eyes. The face outside the iron bars was clearly covered in dark blotches.

When he reached this point in his story, the old man was trembling. I'm telling you all this because I'm old. Despise me if you like, but make sure you write everything down!

I begged him to tell me more about this informer.

My host explained coldly that Teimu Shiad had informed on his friends in return for the school principal's job. He had frequently exchanged tidbits of information for rewards from the secret police. After some years, as some of the imprisoned tribesmen had their sentences commuted and were released, Teimu, terrified of their revenge, had left his school and gone to live deep in the mountains. Avoiding all human contact and breaking off all relations with friends and family, he remained an exile.

Old man, how did you come by all these details? I asked.

Young man, can't you see the dark blotches on my face? I'm that dwarfish, coarse informer, Teimu Shiad. I live here, cut off, imprisoned in the forest, like a Formosan salmon confined to its lonely creek. And it's only by telling you my story this way that I can find the courage to finish it.

Once more, I saw the darkness cross his visage, and knew at last that this was no leafy shadow, but the black marks of inner guilt, timidity, and regret.

I retreated from the seemingly calm center of a raging storm. The salmon in the stream by the roadside seemed strangely agitated as they broke the surface of the water. Reaching my car, I turned to look across the valley and was surprised to see a darkening sky looming over the mountains like an inky-black curtain. The towering peaks, like a row of hunting knives, seemed to sway uneasily.

Dawn was breaking as I drove back to my house in the tribal village. There, news reached us of a great earthquake that had just struck the center of the island. I later read newspaper reports describing how the cliffs from Guguan to Qingshan crumbled from the earthquake, forming a spectacular canyon. It took two years for the Central Highway to open to restricted traffic. Once, passing by the Qingshan Power Plant, I found that the old Japanese-built mountain road was gone. The Tafulan people no longer spoke of the "Son of Bota"; the old man had also disappeared without a trace.

Disasters create memories; they also destroy them. That is why I have written this story.

About the Authors

Wu Zhuoliu (1900–1976), a novelist and journalist, wrote poetry that earned him the reputation of an "iron-willed poet." A prolific writer, Wu was best known for his portrayals of social change in the realist vein. His early works are set in the Japanese colonial era, best represented by the novel *Orphans of Asia*. "Potsdam Section Chief" is his signature piece of the later period, on post-war Taiwanese society.

Ye Shitao (1925–2008) was a writer of fiction, criticism, and essays, as well as a translator. In 1951, he was charged with "not reporting known communists" and imprisoned for five years. He believed that Taiwanese literature reflected conditions on the island, as well as its people's life and writers willing to join the fight for freedom and democracy. His *A History of Taiwan Literature* (translated into English by Christopher Lupke; Cambria Press, 2020), the first of its kind, is written from a Taiwanese perspective.

Lay Chih-ying (1980–) gained recognition while still an undergraduate in college for his short stories, some of which won prizes in Taiwan. With a doctoral degree in agricultural science from McGill University in Canada, he is currently a researcher at the University of Montreal. Lai is most adept at avant-garde, experimental fiction, and complex character portrayals, with a continuing expansion of narrative styles

and subject matters.

Li Ang (1952–), pen name of Shih Shu-tuan, is best known for *The Butcher's Wife*, an indictment of patriarchy, domestic abuse, and societal pressure for gender conformity. Since publishing her first short story at the age of sixteen, Li Ang has never stopped writing or drawing the ire of moralists in Taiwan. An astute observer of cultural and social conditions, she is innovative not only in theme but also in narrative technique.

Her work is widely read around the world, especially in Europe and Japan. In 2004 she was honored by the French Ministry of Culture and Communication with its Chevalier de L'Ordre des Arts et des Lettres; one of her stories has been adapted into a theatrical production in Germany and was a finalist for the Faust Prize. Xie Xuehong's story is one of Li Ang's major works dealing with historical events and personages.

Lee Yu (1944–2014) was a novelist and scholar of art. She earned a doctoral degree in art history from the University of California at Berkeley. A participant in the "Defend the Diaoyu Island Movement" in the 1970s, she was blacklisted, along with her husband, also an accomplished writer, Guo Songfen, and forbidden from entering Taiwan during the martial law era. Her writings are highly modernistic, of which "Nocturnal Strings" is a representative work.

Walis Nokan (1961–), an Atayal writer, was born in the Mihu settlement of Heping Township, Taichung. He began creative writing as a student in a teacher's college. After reading the work of Wu Sheng, a Taiwanese poet, he adopted a realistic writing style and, starting in 1983, published works under the pen name of Liu Ao. In recent years he has focused on promoting Yuanzhumin culture, starting a magazine in 1990 and setting up a research center in 1992. His works, including poetry and reportage, have won many prizes in Taiwan. The stories included in this collection exemplify his talent in reportage literature and his realist approach, while incorporating supernatural and satirical elements.

About the Editors and Translators

Howard Goldblatt is Emeritus Professor of East Asian Languages at the University of Colorado, subsequently Research Professor at the University of Notre Dame. A Guggenheim Fellow and founding editor of the journal *Modern Chinese Literature*, he has received honorary degrees from Hong Kong and British universities. Author or editor of more than a dozen books, in Chinese and English, he is the translator of more than fifty Chinese-language books, including ten by the 2012 Nobel Laureate Mo Yan, and two winners of the Asian Booker Prize. He has co-translated nearly two dozen with Sylvia Li-chun Lin, one the winner of the Asian Booker, another recipient of the Translation of the Year Award from the American Literary Translators Association. He has published a collection of flash fiction entitled *A Night in a Chinese Hospital*.

Sylvia Li-chun Lin, a native of Tainan, Taiwan, earned a doctoral degree in Comparative Literature from the University of California at Berkeley. She was Associate Professor of Chinese at the University of Notre Dame before resigning to become a full-time translator and writer. Author of *Representing Atrocity in Taiwan: The 2/28 Incident and White Terror in Fiction and Film*, she is professionally and personally invested in fictional works dealing with this part of Taiwan's past. She coedited *Documenting Taiwan on Film: issues and Methods in New Documentaries*. Besides translating fiction from Chinese, she is also writing a series of essays on food in cross-cultural exchanges.

Dafydd Fell is the Reader in Comparative Politics with special reference to Taiwan at the Department of Politics and International Studies of the School of Oriental and African Studies (SOAS), University of London. He is also the Director of the SOAS Centre of Taiwan Studies. He has published numerous articles on political parties and electioneering in Taiwan. His books include *Party Politics in Taiwan* (Routledge, 2005),

Government and Politics in Taiwan (Routledge, 2011) and the second edition was published in early 2018. He coedited *Migration to and from Taiwan* (Routledge, 2013) and his next edited volume, *Social Movements in Taiwan under Ma Ying-jeou* (Routledge) was published in 2017. His most recent coedited book was *Taiwan Studies Revisited*, published in 2019.

Chris Wen-Chao Li received his doctorate in general linguistics and comparative philology from Oxford University and currently teaches linguistics and translation/interpretation at San Francisco State University. He is the author of *A Diachronically-Motivated Segmental Phonology of Mandarin Chinese* and *The Routledge Course in Chinese Media Literacy*. His writings have appeared in such scholarly journals as *Language and Communication, Diaspora Studies*, and *Target*, while his translations have been published in *Renditions, The Chinese Pen*, and *Asia Pacific Translation and Intercultural Studies*.

Jewel Lo studied Economics for her BA degree at Chinese Culture University and received her MSc Degree in Computer Science from the University of Leeds. In Taiwan she has worked in trading companies, language schools and local radio. After moving to the United Kingdom she has worked in the international higher education sector and at the SOAS Centre of Taiwan Studies.

Craig A. Smith is a lecturer of translation studies at the University of Melbourne. He holds a PhD from the University of British Columbia and an MA from National Chung Cheng University. He has recently published the coedited volume *Translating the Occupation: The Japanese Invasion of China, 1931-45* and his articles have appeared in journals such as *Modern Chinese Literature and Culture, Modern Asian Studies*, and *Twentieth-Century China*. His first monograph, *Chinese Asianism*, will be published by the Harvard University Asia Center in 2021.

Darryl Sterk teaches translation at Lingnan University. He holds a PhD and an MA from the University of Toronto and a BA from the University of Alberta. Dr. Sterk's *Indigenous Cultural Translation: A Thick Description of* Seediq Bale will be published in 2020. He has published in *Modern Chinese Literatures and Cultures*. He is a literary translator. His translation of Wu Ming-Yi's *The Stolen Bicycle* was longlisted for the Booker International in 2017.

Edward Vickers is Professor of Comparative Education at Kyushu University, Japan. He holds a PhD from the University of Hong Kong, and an MA and a BA in Modern History from the University of Oxford. Professor Vickers' publications include *Education and Society in Post-Mao China*, *Remembering Asia's World War Two*, and *In Search of An Identity: The Politics of History as a School Subject in Hong Kong, 1960s-2005*. He is Director of the Kyushu University Taiwan Program, and Secretary-General of the Comparative Education Society of Asia.

Cambria Literature in Taiwan Series

General Editor: Nikky Lin
(National Taiwan Normal University)

A Taiwanese Literature Reader edited by Nikky Lin

The Soul of Jade Mountain by Husluman Vava, translated by Terence Russell

A History of Taiwan Literature by Ye Shitao, translated by Christopher Lupke

A Son of Taiwan: Stories of Government Atrocity edited by Howard Goldblatt and Sylvia Li-chun Lin

Transitions in Taiwan: Stories of the White Terror edited by Ian Rowen

Queer Taiwanese Literature: A Reader edited by Howard Chiang

www.ingramcontent.com/pod-product-compliance
Lightning Source LLC
Chambersburg PA
CBHW031833230426
43669CB00009B/1338